AF327222

JOEL SHAPIRO

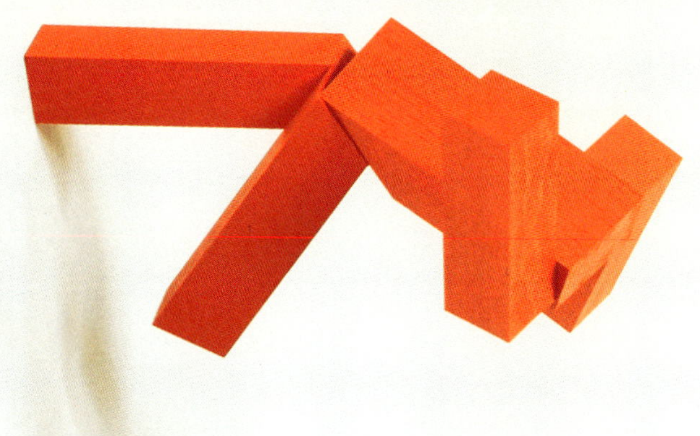

JOEL SHAPIRO

NEW WOOD AND BRONZE SCULPTURE

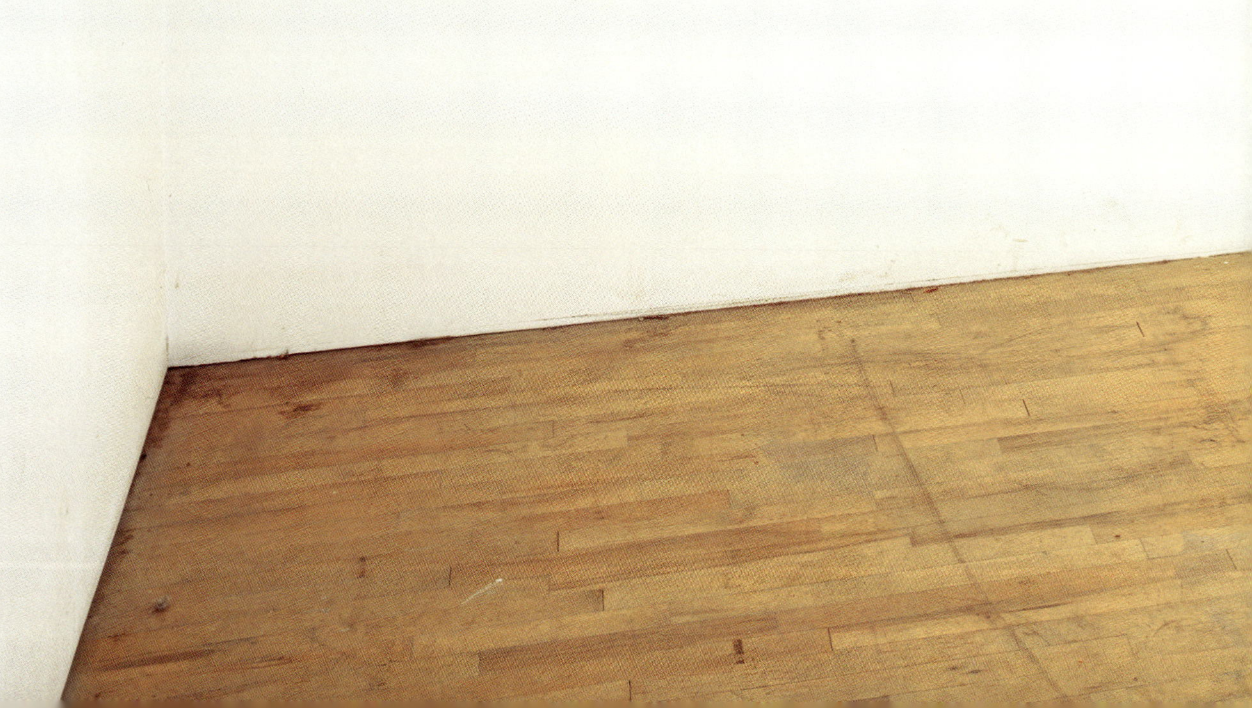

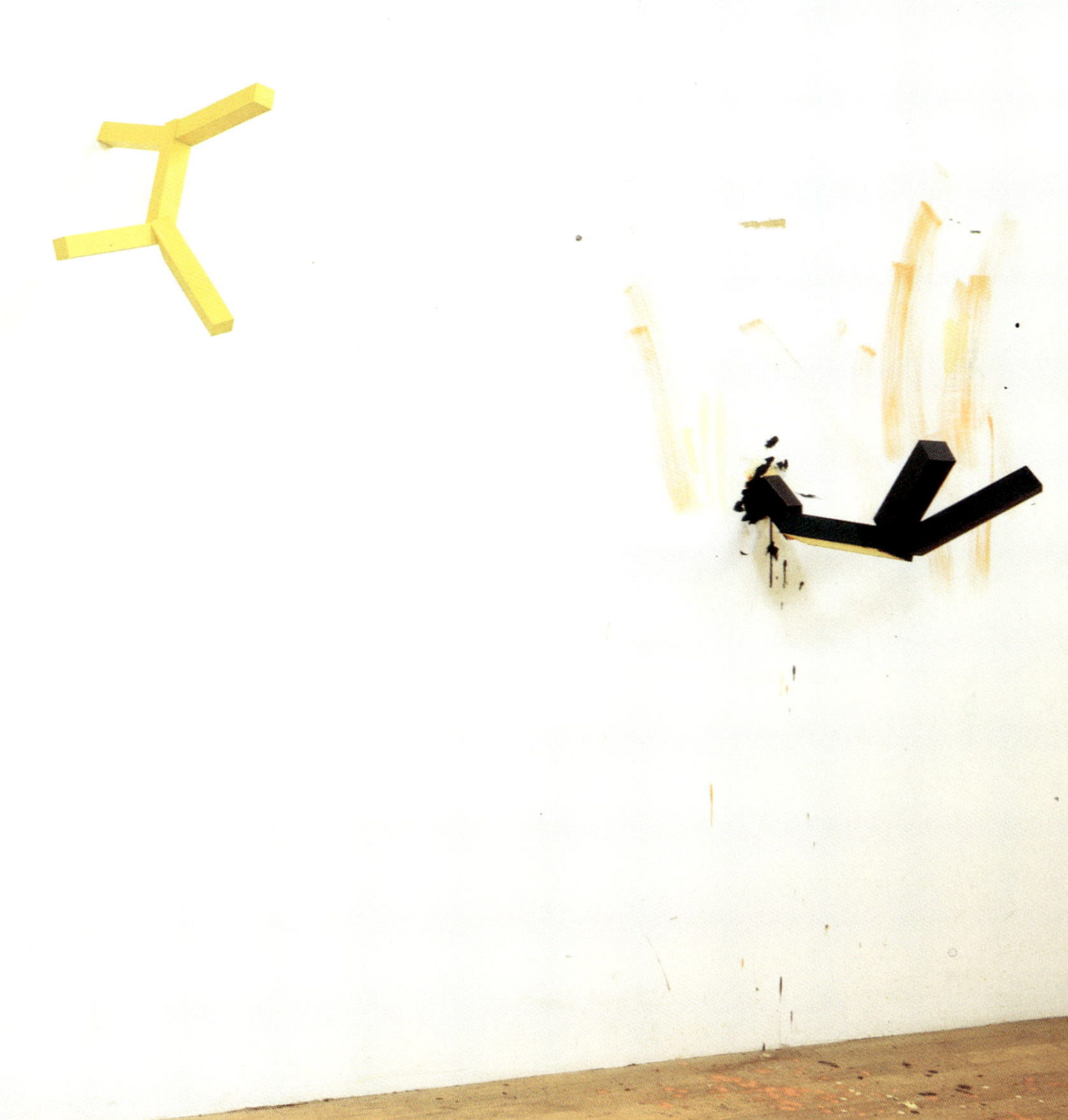

October 16 - November 14, 1998

32 East 57th Street New York City
142 Greene Street New York City

PACEWILDENSTEIN

Dancing with Gravity

Klaus Kertess

Whether Joel Shapiro's artmaking humanizes geometry or dehumanizes the figure is moot. Depending upon the viewer's movement, Shapiro's sculpture shifts from the abstract to the figurative, from hyperkinetic flight to collapse, from purely formal to deeply emotional—like a kaleidoscope whose pieces promise, but finally refuse, to settle into resolution. The visually precarious angles at which the rectangular blocks configuring his sculpture are joined seem to set off a chain reaction of disjunctions—physical and psychological. The only certainty is the dynamic body given to ambiguity.

The simple blocks configuring Shapiro's highly crafted, human-scale, stickmanlike sculpture hark back to the exuberant innocence of childhood play as much as to the scholastic severities of Minimalism's monadic geometries, out of which his sculpture developed and against which it reacted. Shapiro was one of the first artists, in the 1970s, to retrieve the technique of casting that had been rejected by late modernism and also to reinfuse his forms with the kind of complex inner life consciously drained from the repetitive units and simple arithmetic progressions of the self-contained objecthood so prevalent in the sculpture of the 1960s.

Minimalism's rigorously pared-down forms and conceptual stringency were critical to Shapiro's beginnings, but he prefers Tony Smith's irregular botanized geometry to the non-referentiality of Donald Judd's geometry. He is an admirer (and collector) of Southeast Asian sculpture, which is so often characterized by a lush restraint of form and volume that gives the breath of spiritual repose—even when consummating serpentine sexual contortions. While this sensuous serenity may be foreign to our culture, Shapiro's balletic geometries have been informed by the formal economy and acute expressiveness of bodily gesture common to disparate Southeast Asian sculpture, whether pre-Khmer Cambodian stone pieces or the Chola bronzes of southern India. Closer to home is the simultaneously dignified and traumatized repose of Alberto Giacometti's figures, so afflicted with implosions of mortality. Similarly dignified and indignified are Shapiro's sculptures as they grapple with the state of rectangularity.

The totally inorganic shape of the rectangle is a unique invention of humankind that, of course, became the most ubiquitous form in urban, industrial culture, from temple to domestic dwelling to skyscraper to box to movie screen to book to refrigerator to Piet Mondrian's quest for spiritual essence to Ad Reinhardt's quest for art's essence of art to postage stamps—and more and more and more. Shapiro's brilliance resides in his ability to make his accumulation of rectangular units articulate that wavering edge where the assertion of inner self and overwhelming public standardization meet. Since the late 1970s, he has primarily devoted his artmaking to quasi-figurative formations of brave formal and psychological vulnerability. His most recent work, in both bronze and wood, speeds perilously close to collapse, frequently confounding the viewer's kinesthetic responses to his human-scale rectangular gymnastics by incorporating more limbs than can be anthropomorphically anticipated. One 1997 untitled bronze (p. 13) is now desperately distended across 21 feet of kneeling and flailing figure-likeness in a painful fall, now a dynamically torqued abstraction of intersecting L-configurations, now gliding forward ecstatically like an enraptured skater with one leg raised back—but, no, the grounded leg of the skater has an anatomically impossible extension, and a double rectangle too large to be read as a head extends defiantly from what only moments ago was perceived as the body's torso. No view is favored, no view is correct, no view is complete. As the sculpture struggles for resolution in space, so too does the viewer. Viewer and viewed choreograph one another, mutually striving for a unity impossible to attain but necessary to attempt—a startling duet of mortality.

Gravity is the sculpture's mortality—grounding its materiality, imposing restraints upon its aspirations to ascend, constantly threatening its balance with collapse, limiting its thrust. And, more clearly and precariously than ever before, these recent sculptures make dramatically visual the interaction of body language and abstract, formal language as it is being grammaticized by gravity.

The bronze sculptures are cast from wood, and their metal surface bears the traces of the wood's grain; the casting process thus replaces the vulnerable wood with an impermeable public armor. Shapiro's structuring is not predetermined; he and an assistant spend painstaking hours adjusting the balance of the initially desired configuration—adding and subtracting prosthetic-like limbs that enable the sculpture's tenuous freestandingness. The more extreme distensions and contortions performed by the most recent works account for the greater quantity of rectangular limbs and the increase in abstract dynamics. The complex process of achieving balance has now been made more visible and visceral.

There are, as well, those sculptures that achieve their final state in the medium of wood—often but not always with the addition of color intuitively tuned to the psychoformal intentions of that particular work. In one of the most process-revealing and psychologically excruciating of his recent sculptures, Shapiro suspended a figure-like structure with limbs akimbo and one potential arm still detached to struggle in an improvisatory scaffold extending from and built around it. The figure is at once entrapped and given the potential of movement by this web of rectangularity. In another wood sculpture, the rectangular blocks are connected but not actually joined together by metal rods, one group hanging from the ceiling above a second group propped up on the floor, giving the appearance of a suspended marionette awaiting the call to unity and action. Are these the embodiments of a contemporary sculptor who is simultaneously dependent upon and liberating himself from the modernist grid?

Even when Shapiro's sculpture is attached to the plane of the wall to revel in the space of painting's illusion, its flight, like that of Icarus, is still menaced by gravity. In the sparest of a group of remarkable painted wood wall pieces, a black T-formation (*Untitled*, 1997; p. 32) seems to have been split across its bottom third by gravity and lunges downward, at the waist, like a top-heavy crucified figure. Another work in this painted wood group has a more comically and awkwardly jumbled complex of rectangles that could readily be seen as two figures wrestling and/or engaged in a sexual act, as they careen, oblivious to the dictates of gravity, toward the plane of the floor. Whether in works of this relatively modest size (the largest is about 3 feet long) or far vaster, Shapiro's finely tuned sense of scale, form, and movement propels his sculpture into continuously shifting engagement with the viewer, but never overwhelms with superfluous mass and volume. With this recent work, Shapiro literally and figuratively extends his vocabulary into new acts of movement and moving acts.

Klaus Kertess is a writer and curator. He is currently working on a novel and has curated the Willem de Kooning exhibition, *Drawing Seeing/Seeing Drawing* for the Drawing Center in New York (October 30–December 19, 1998; traveling to the Addison Gallery of American Art, Andover, Massachusetts, and the Wexner Center for the Arts, Columbus, Ohio).

Untitled, 1997, bronze, 87 × 58 $\frac{1}{2}$ × 31 $\frac{1}{2}$", unique

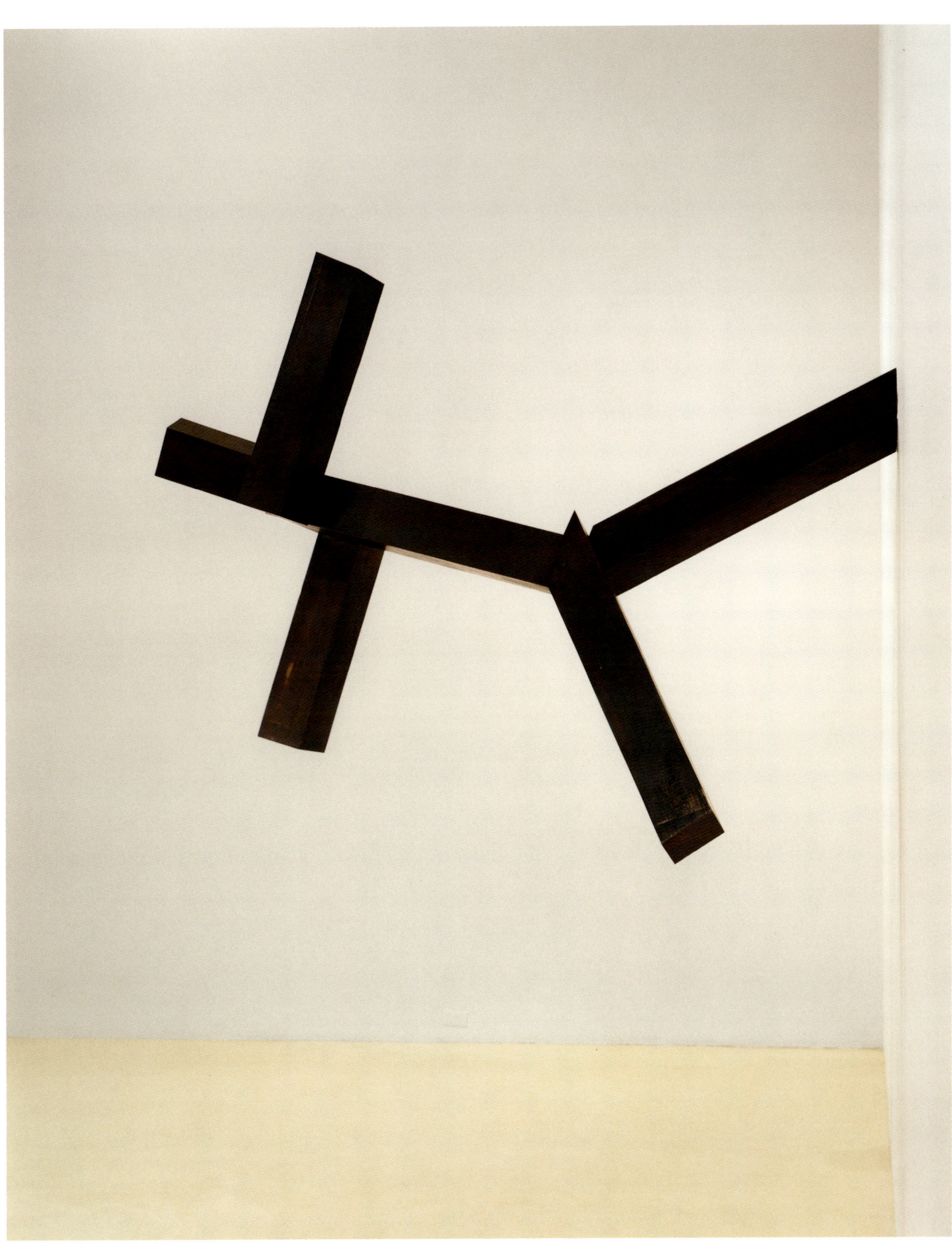

Untitled, 1997, bronze, 8' 6" x 12' x 10', edition 1/2

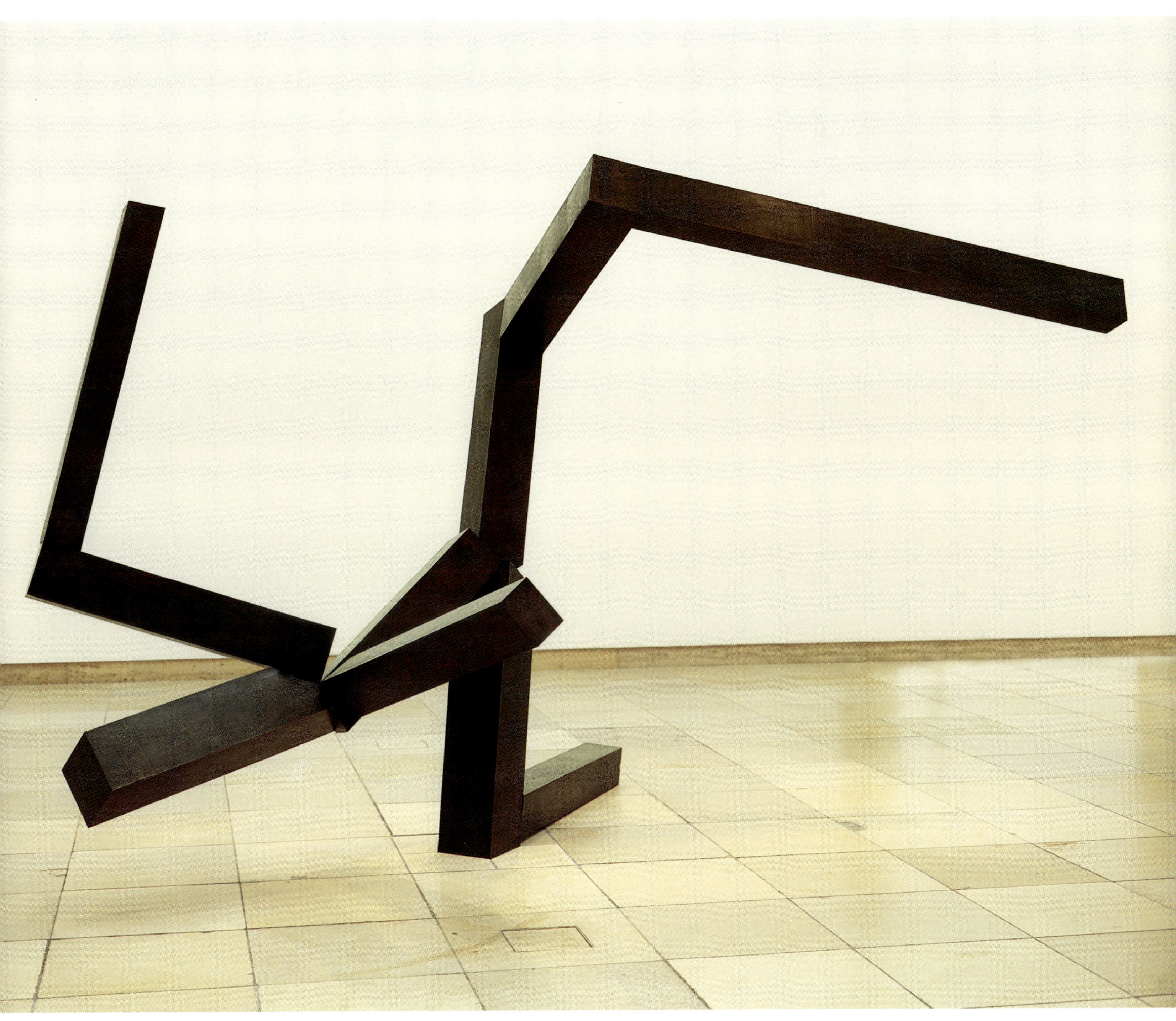

Untitled, 1997, bronze, 10' 6" × 21' 6" × 9', unique

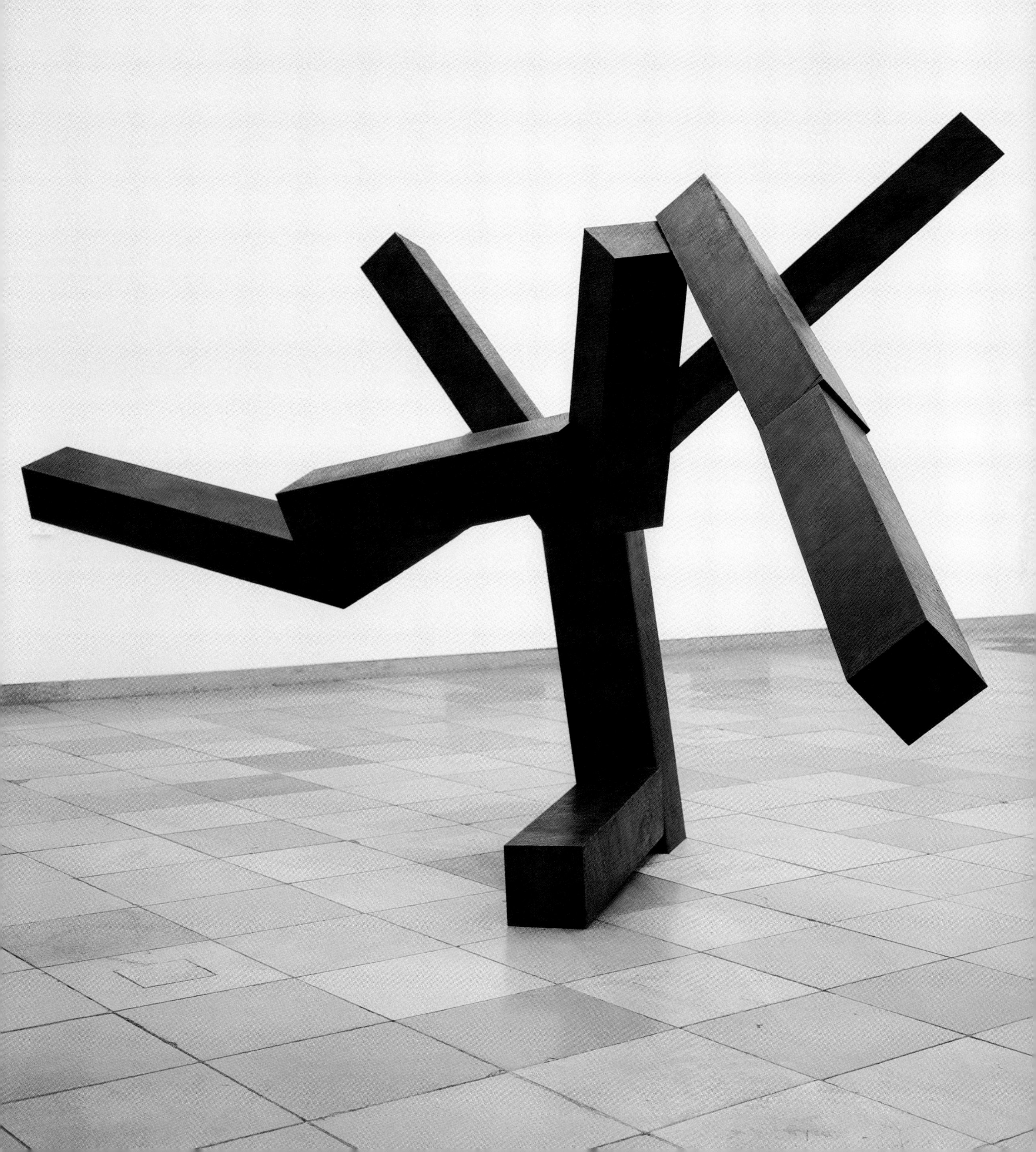

Untitled, 1998, wood and steel, 67 x 24 x 21 1/2" variable

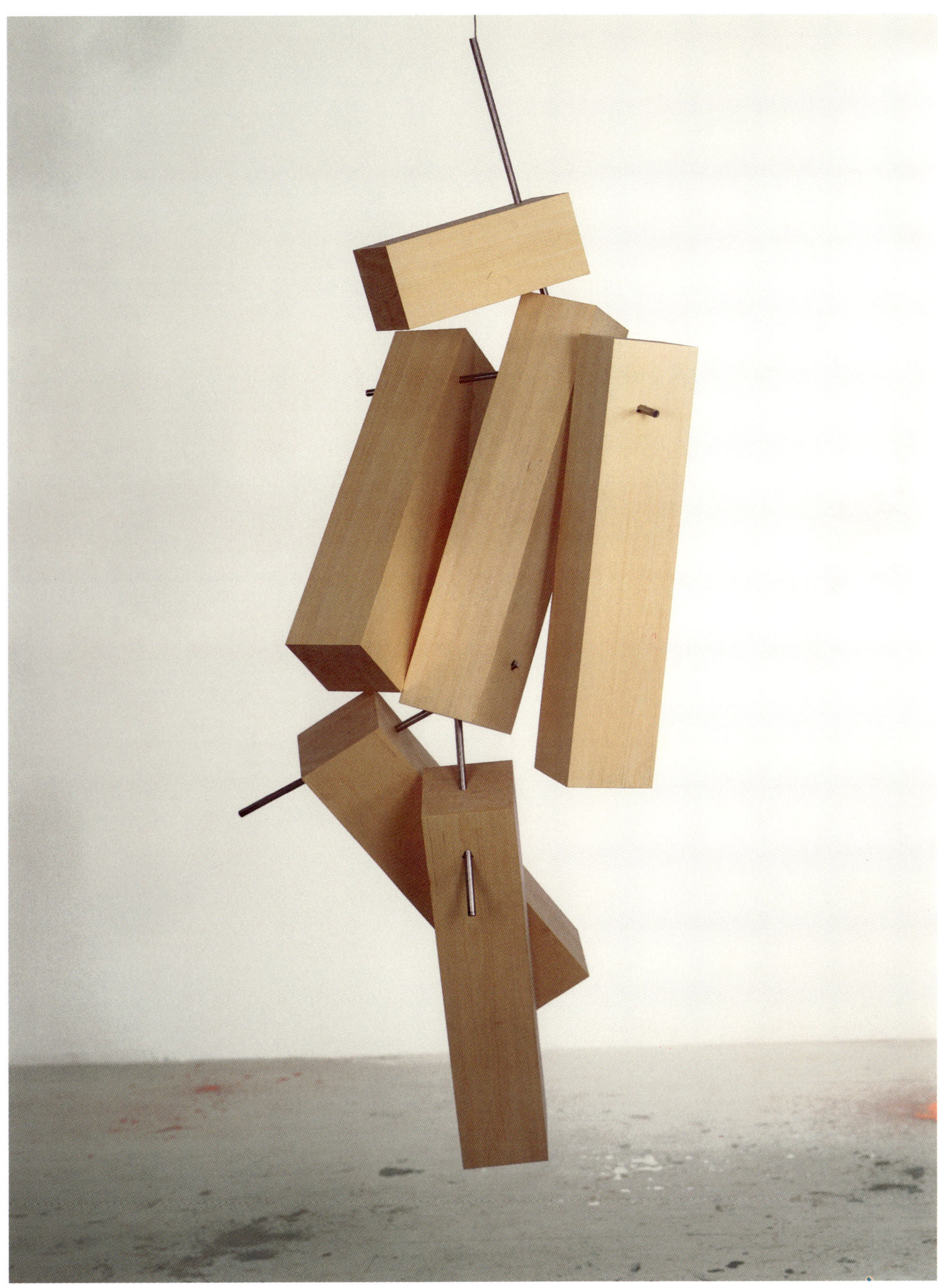

Untitled, 1998, wood and steel, 56 × 27 × 33"

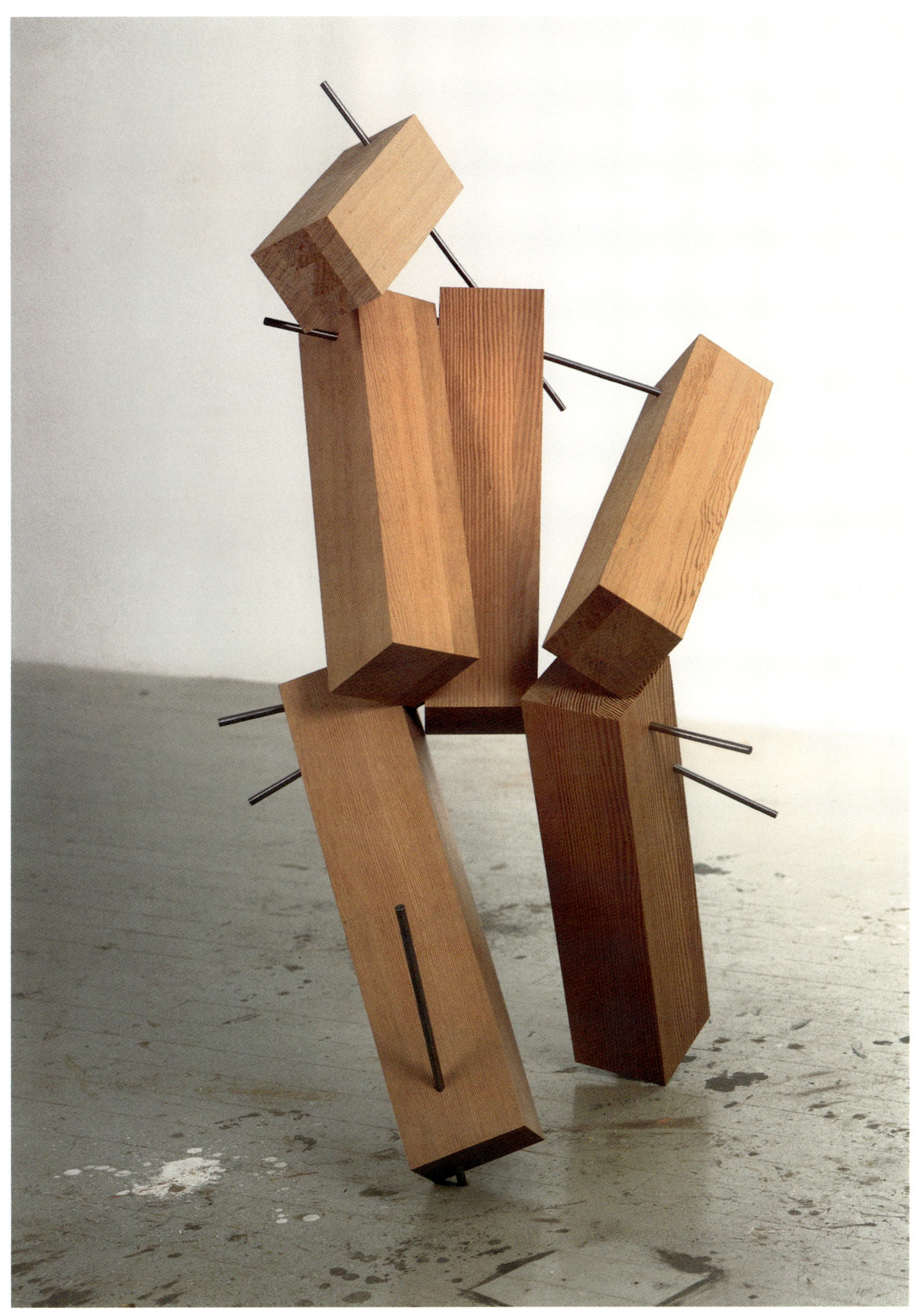

Untitled, 1998, wood and steel, 79 × 58 × 30" variable

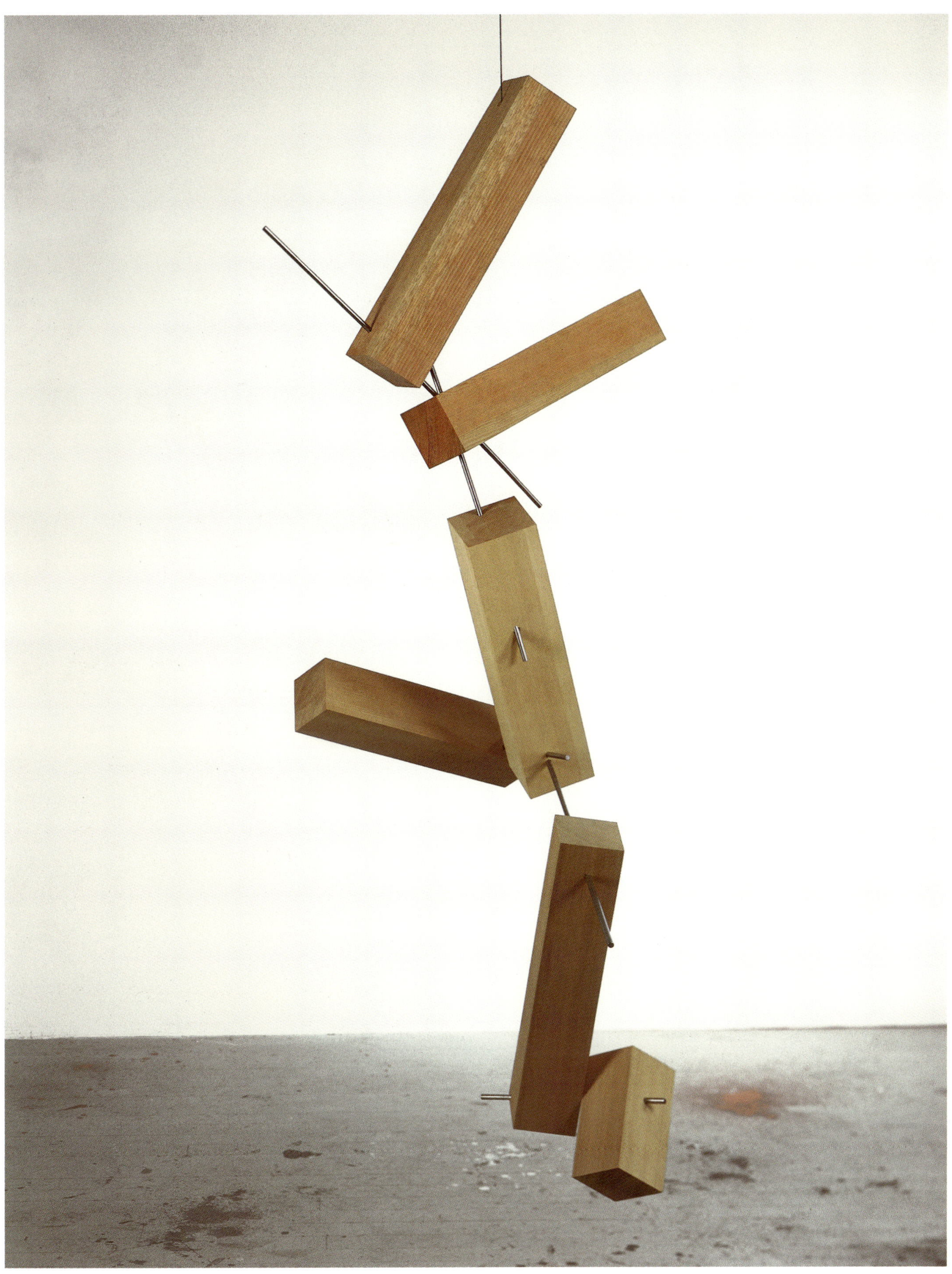

Untitled, 1998, wood, 94 $^1/_2$" x 9' 9" x 8' 2"

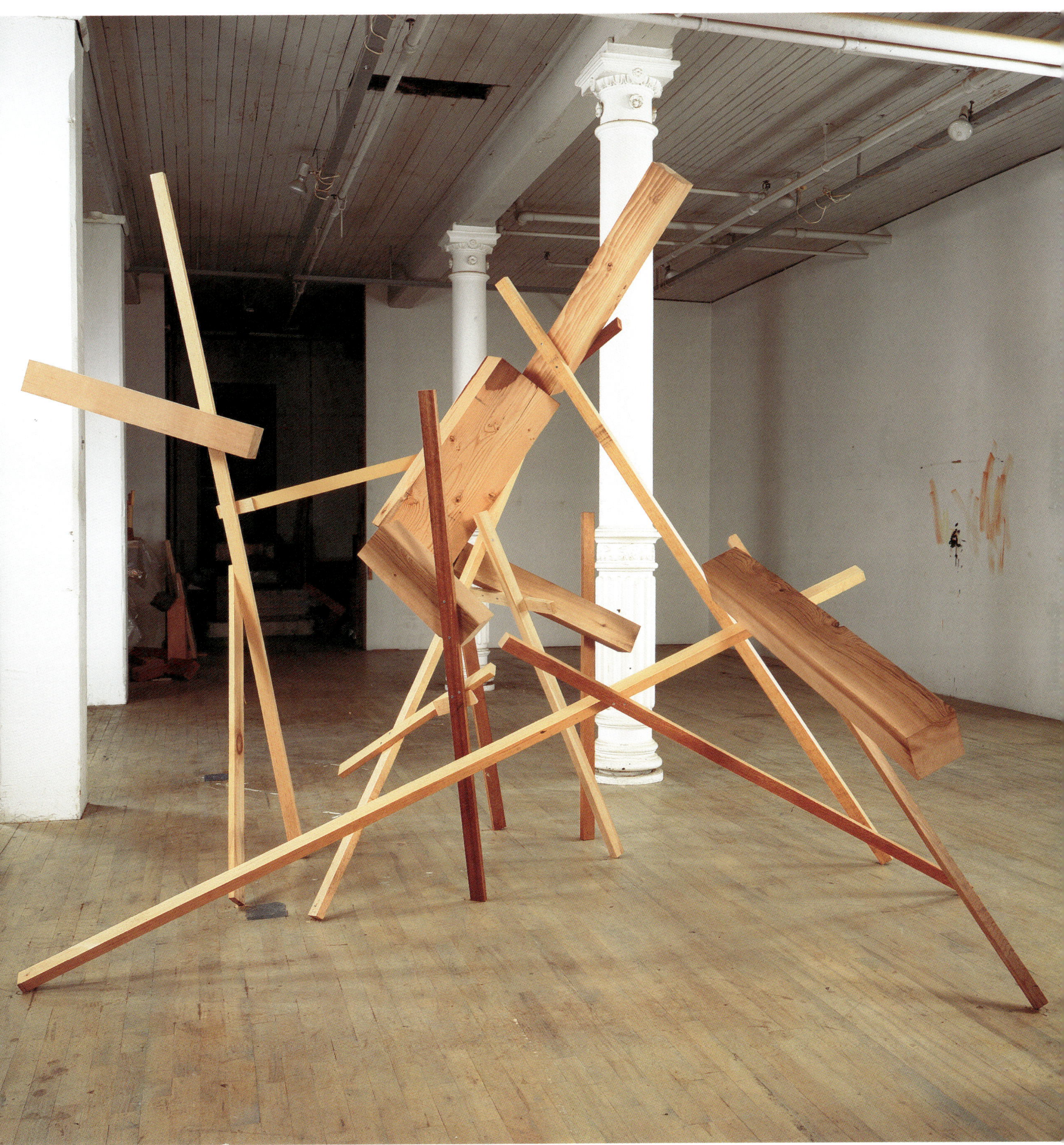

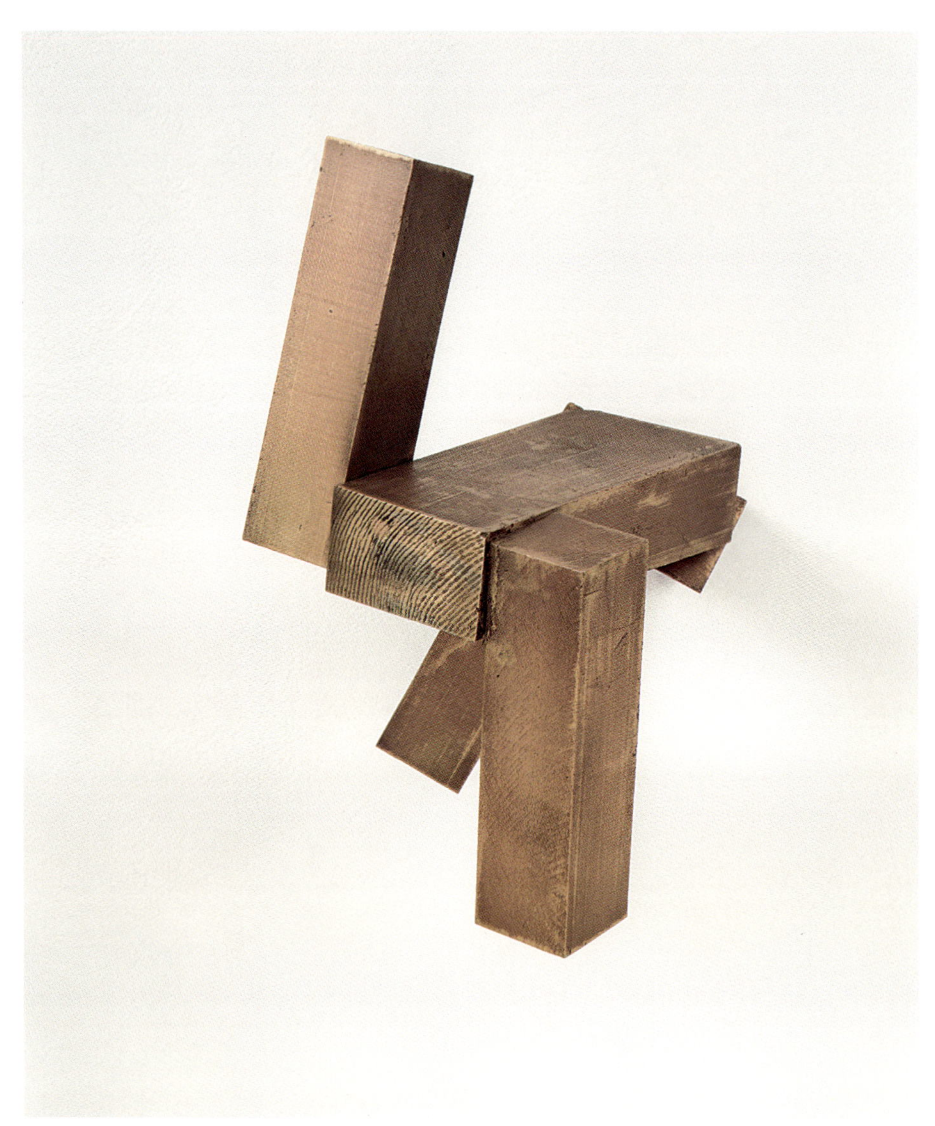

Untitled, 1998, bronze, 15 ¹/₄ × 9 ³/₄ × 16 ³/₈", unique

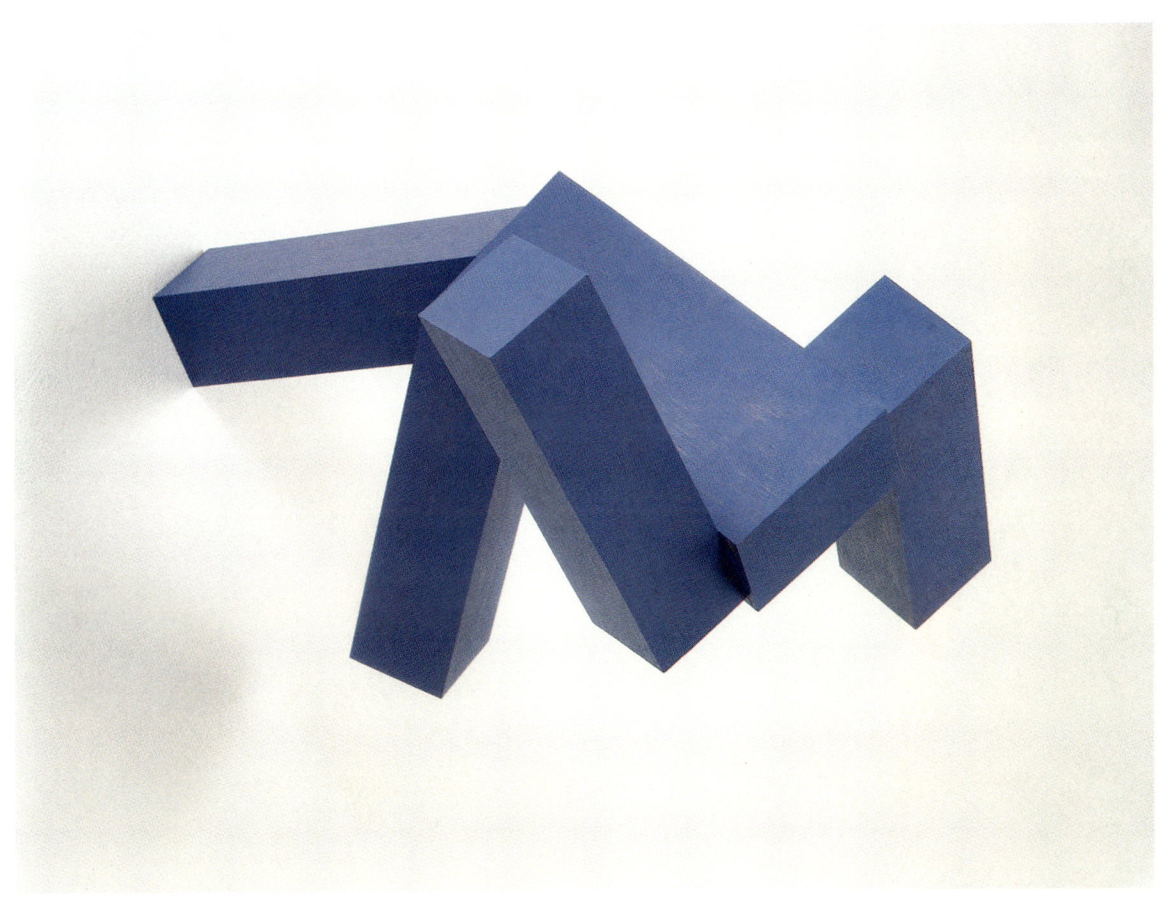

Untitled, 1997, oil paint on wood, 15 × 22 $\frac{1}{2}$ × 25 $\frac{1}{2}$"

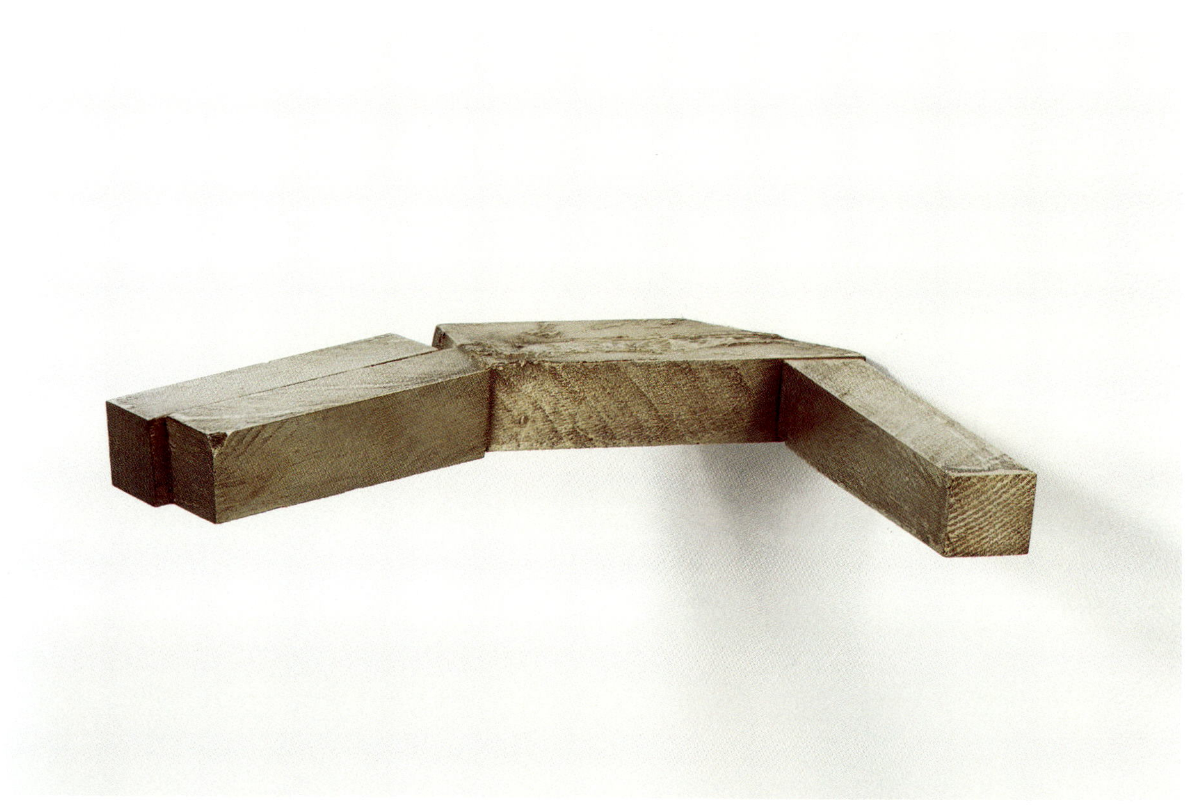

Untitled, 1997-98, bronze, 2 $^3/_8$ × 13 $^1/_2$ × 9 $^1/_2$", unique

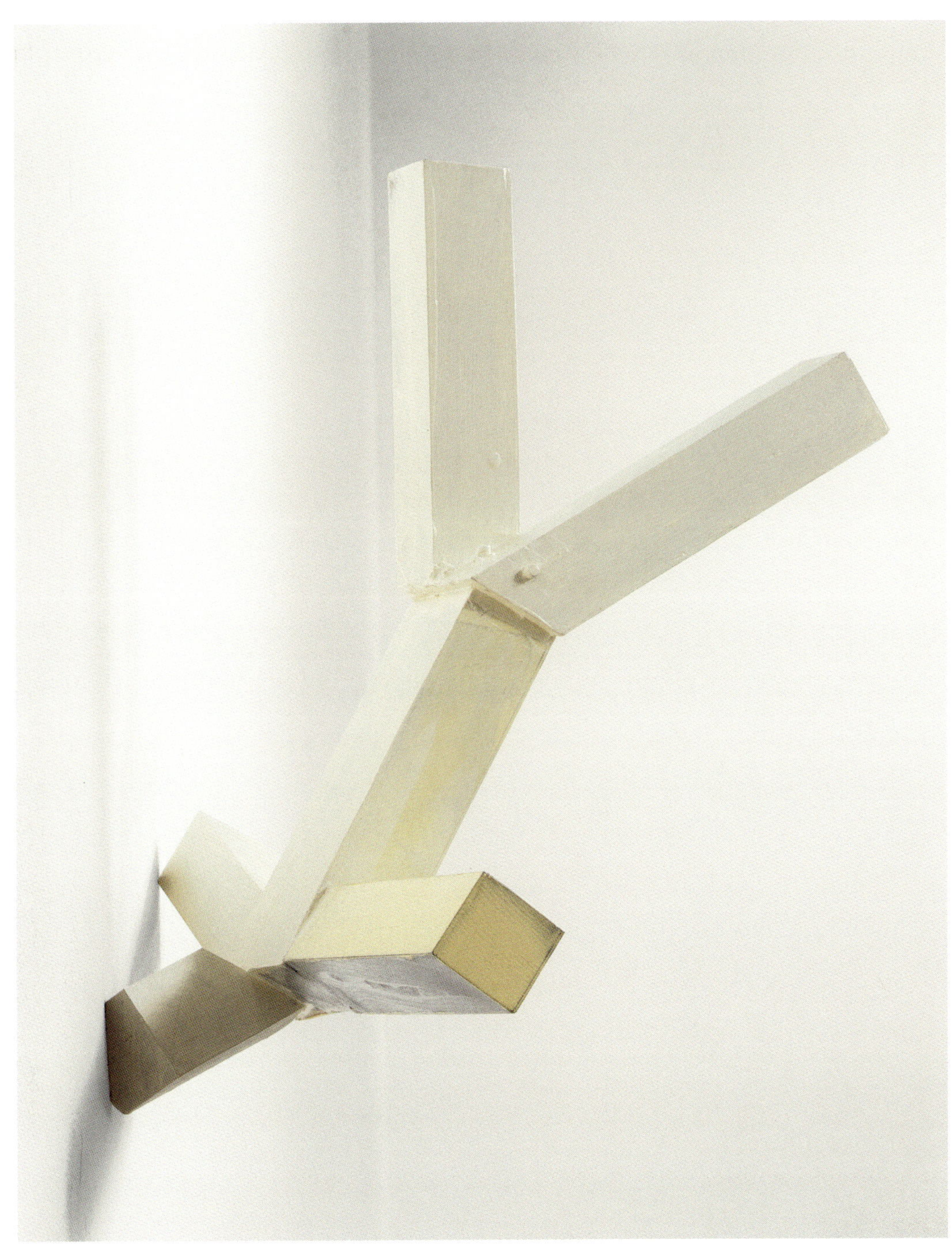

Untitled, 1997, oil paint on aluminum, 18 $^{1}/_{2}$ × 18 $^{1}/_{2}$ × 16 $^{1}/_{4}$"

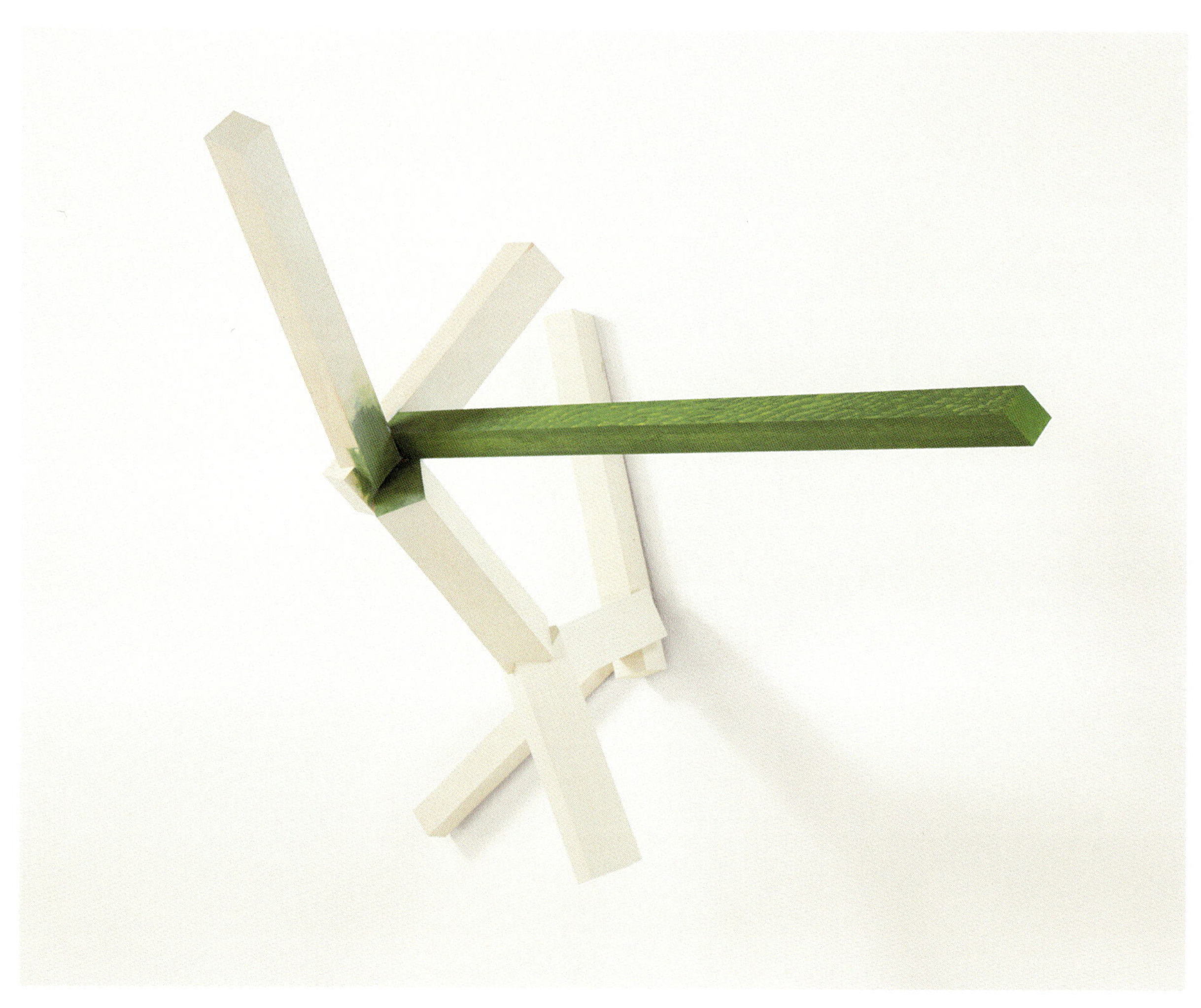

Untitled, 1997-98, oil paint on wood, 30 x 51 ¹/₄ x 39"

Untitled, 1998, cast iron and white bronze
9 x 16 x 18 ¹/₂", cast iron; 9 x 12 ¹/₂ x 18 ¹/₂", white bronze

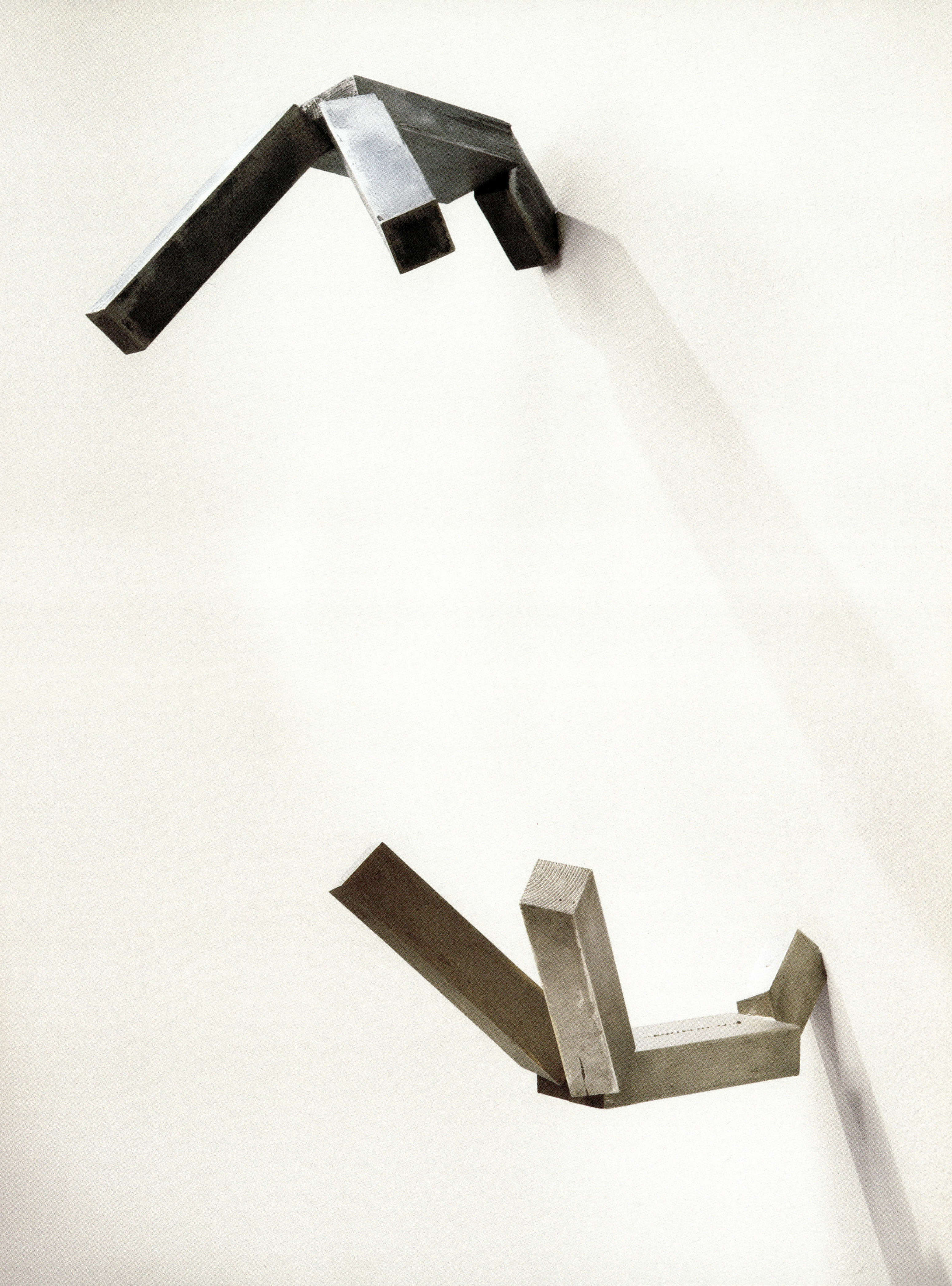

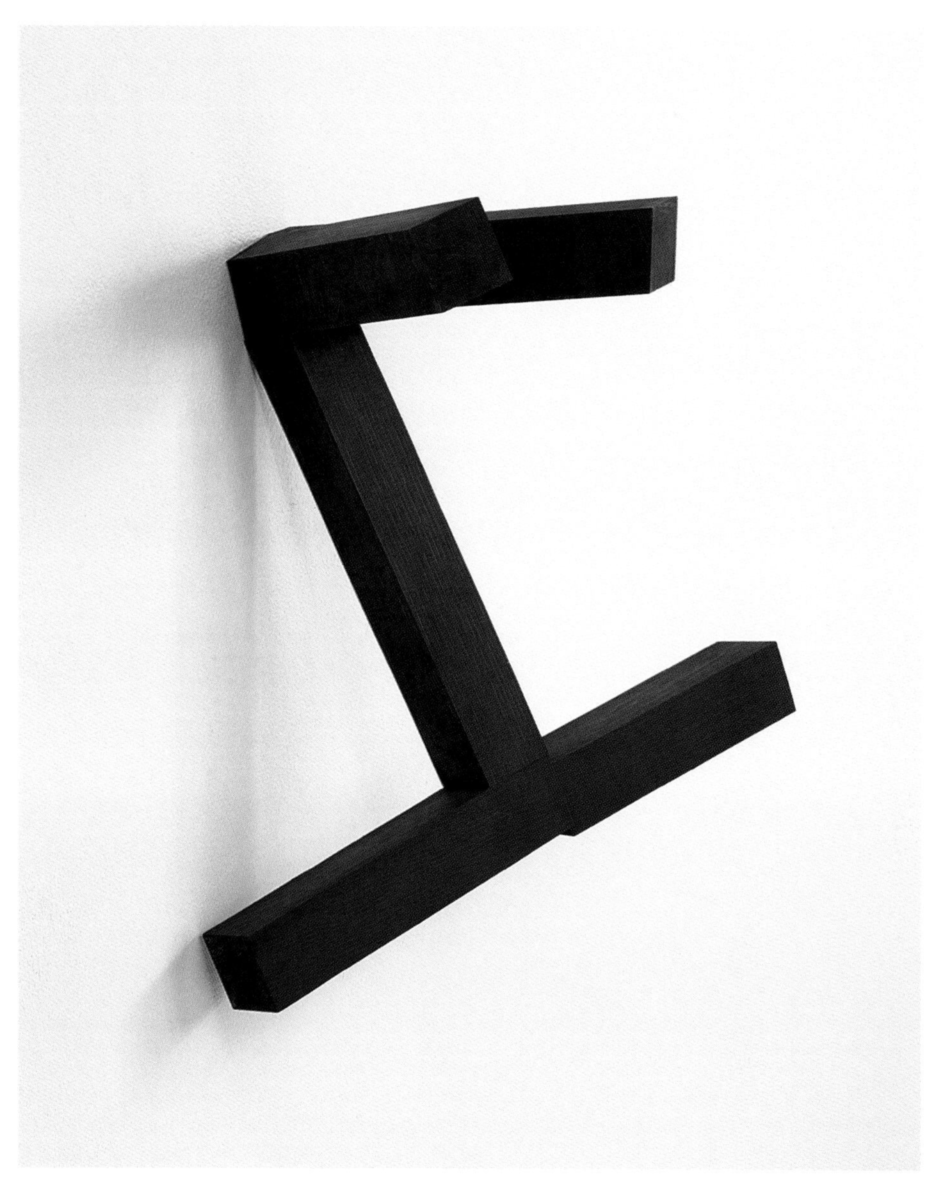

Untitled, 1997, oil paint on wood, 18 ¹/₂ × 17 × 10 ¹/₂"

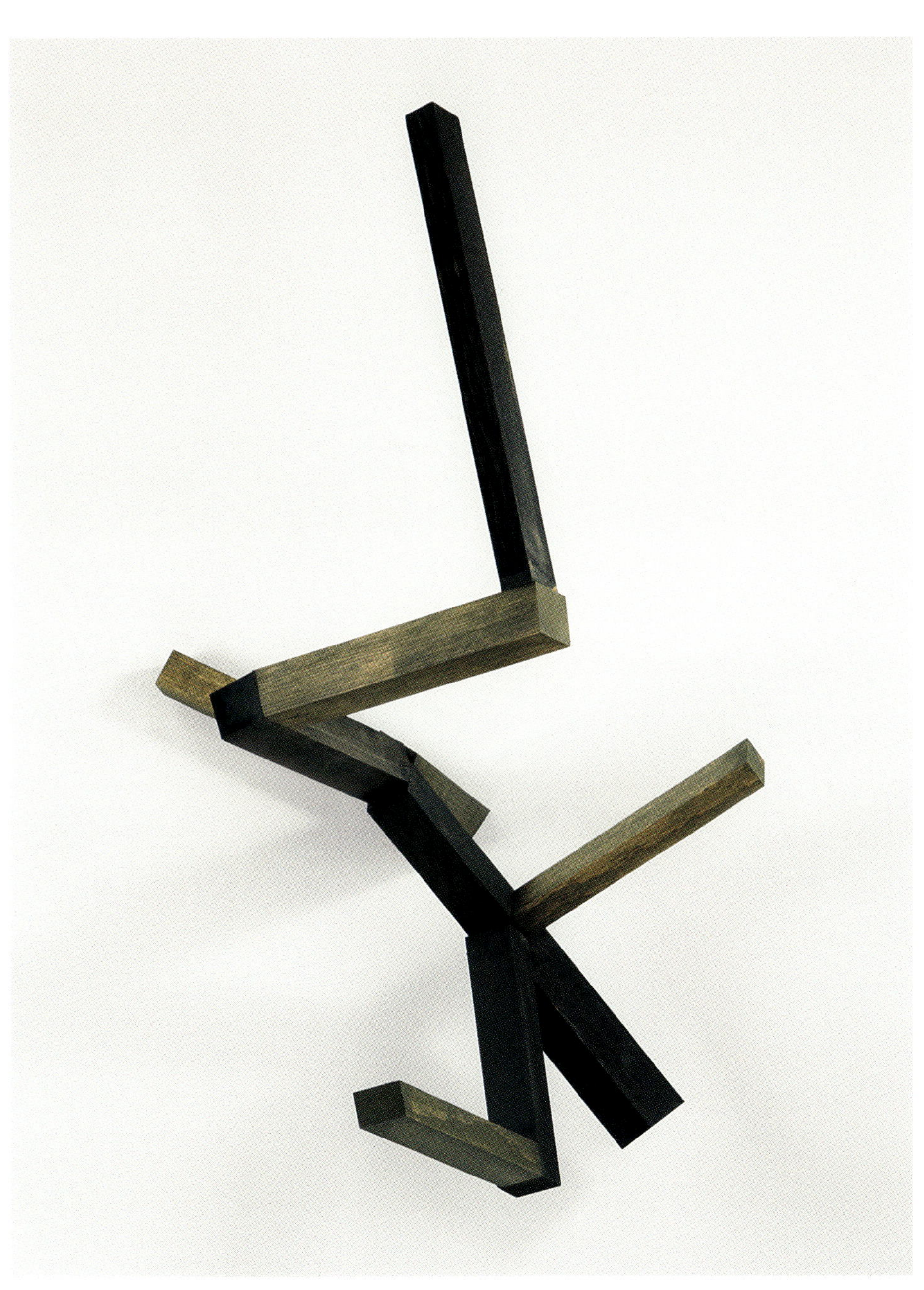

Untitled, 1997, oil paint on wood, 24 $^{1}/_{2}$ × 38 $^{1}/_{2}$ × 24 $^{1}/_{2}$"

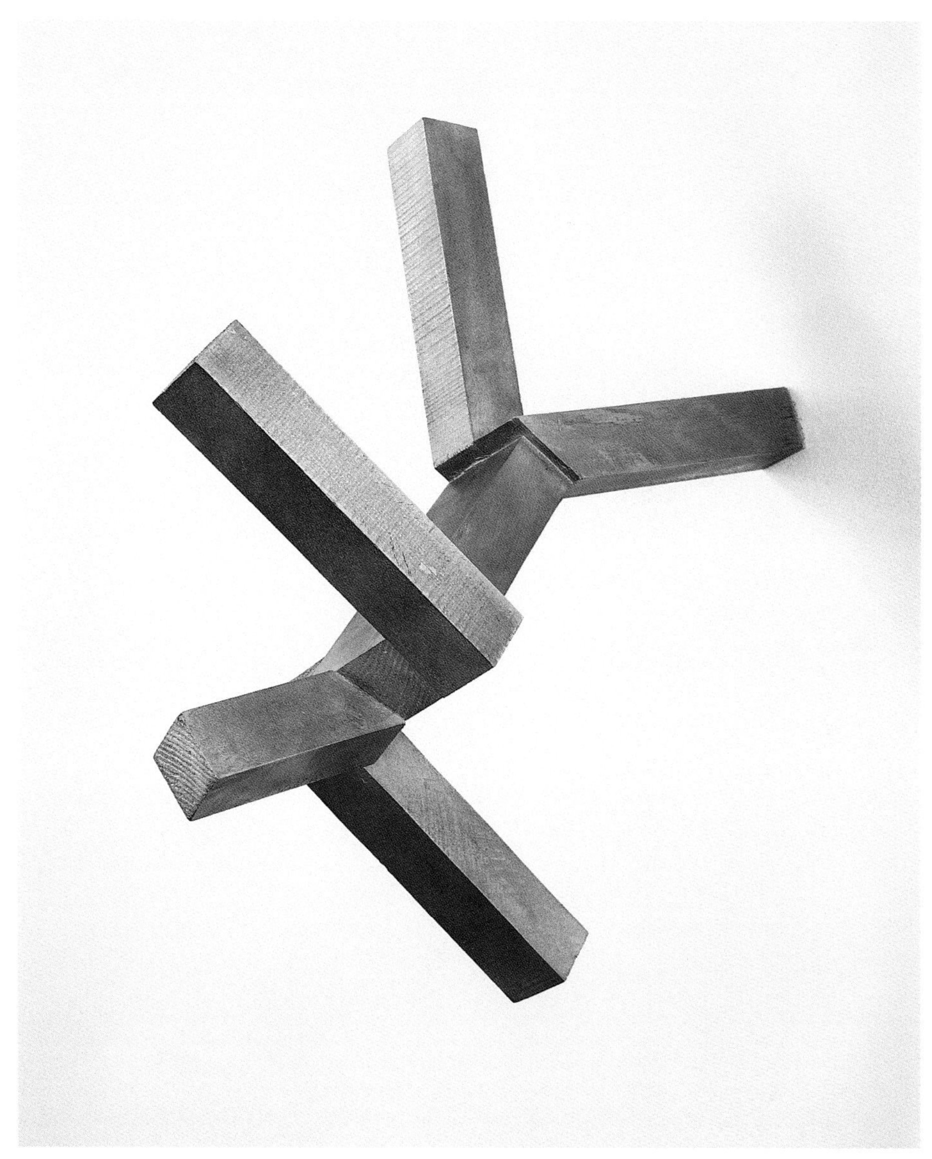

Untitled, 1997, aluminum, 21 × 9 × 20", unique

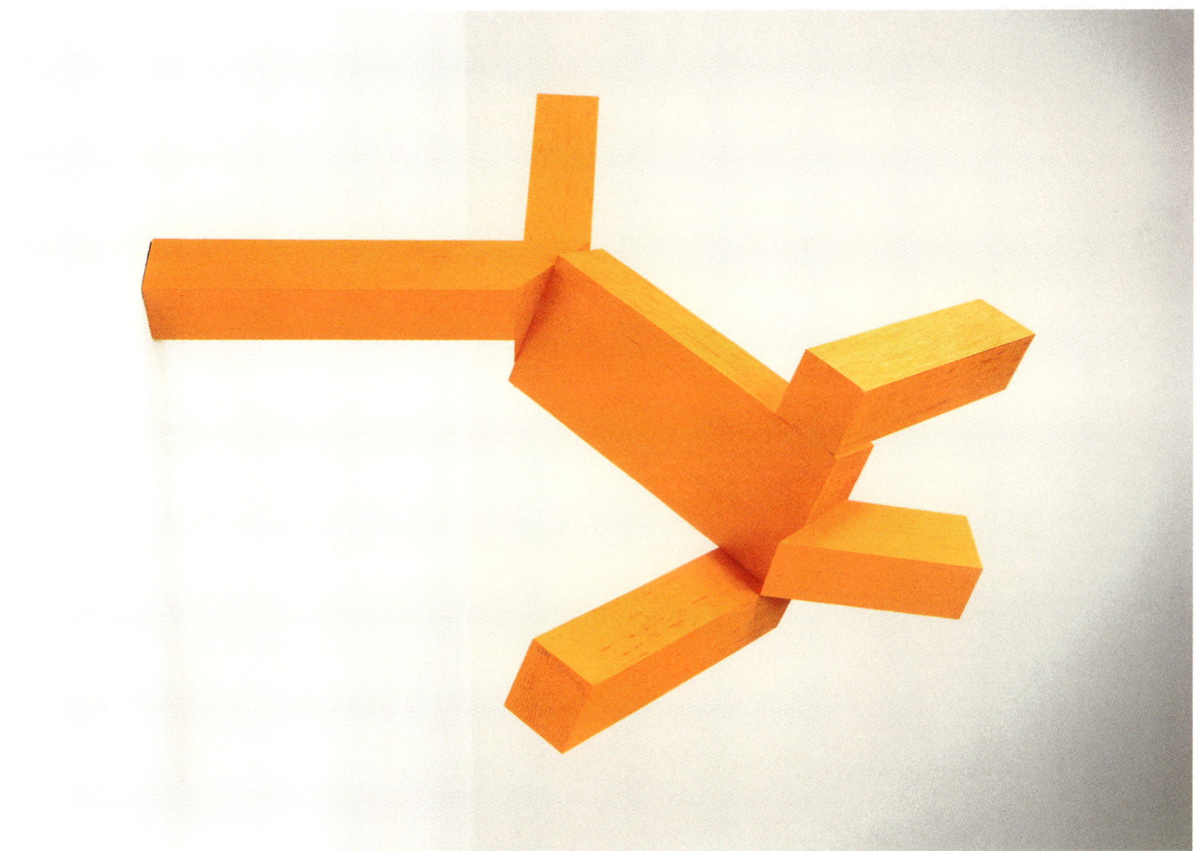

Untitled, 1998, oil paint on wood, 16 3/4 × 13 1/2 × 20 1/2"

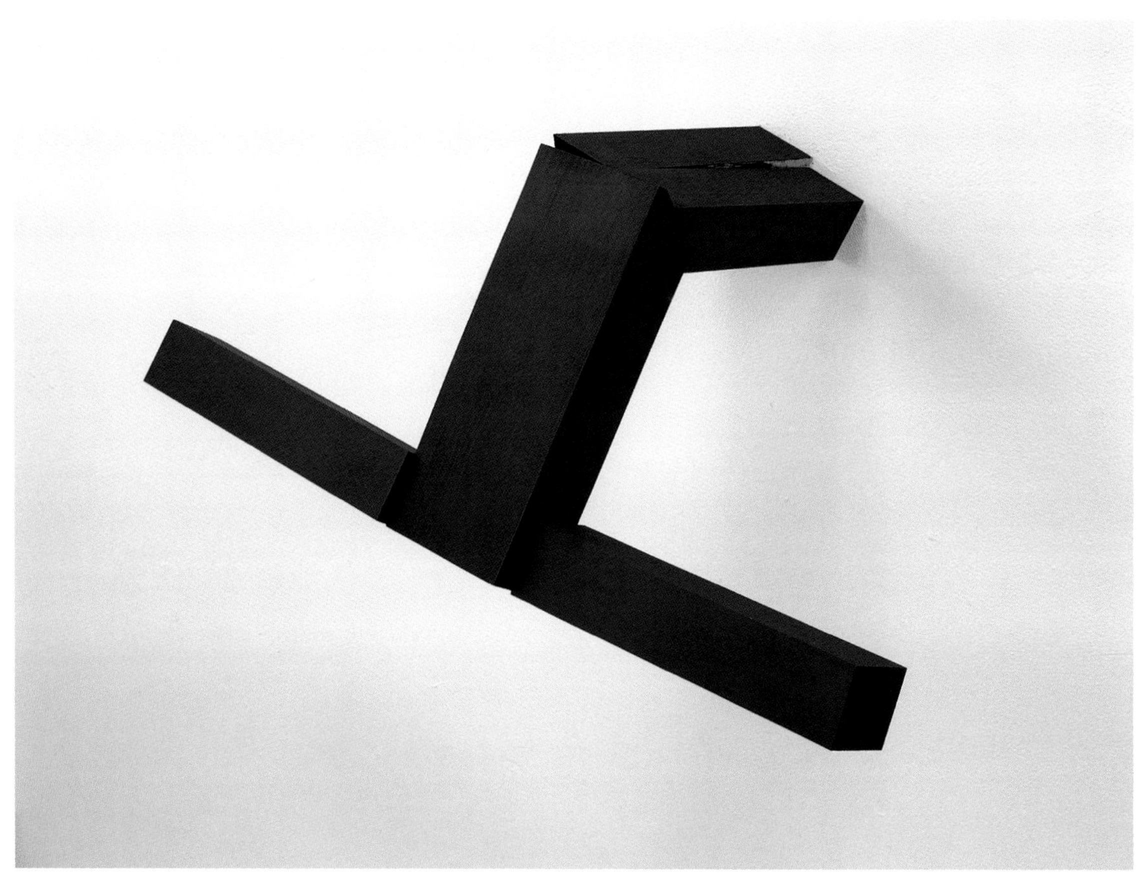

Untitled, 1997, oil paint on wood, 22 $^5/_8$ × 16 $^3/_8$ × 17 $^3/_8$"

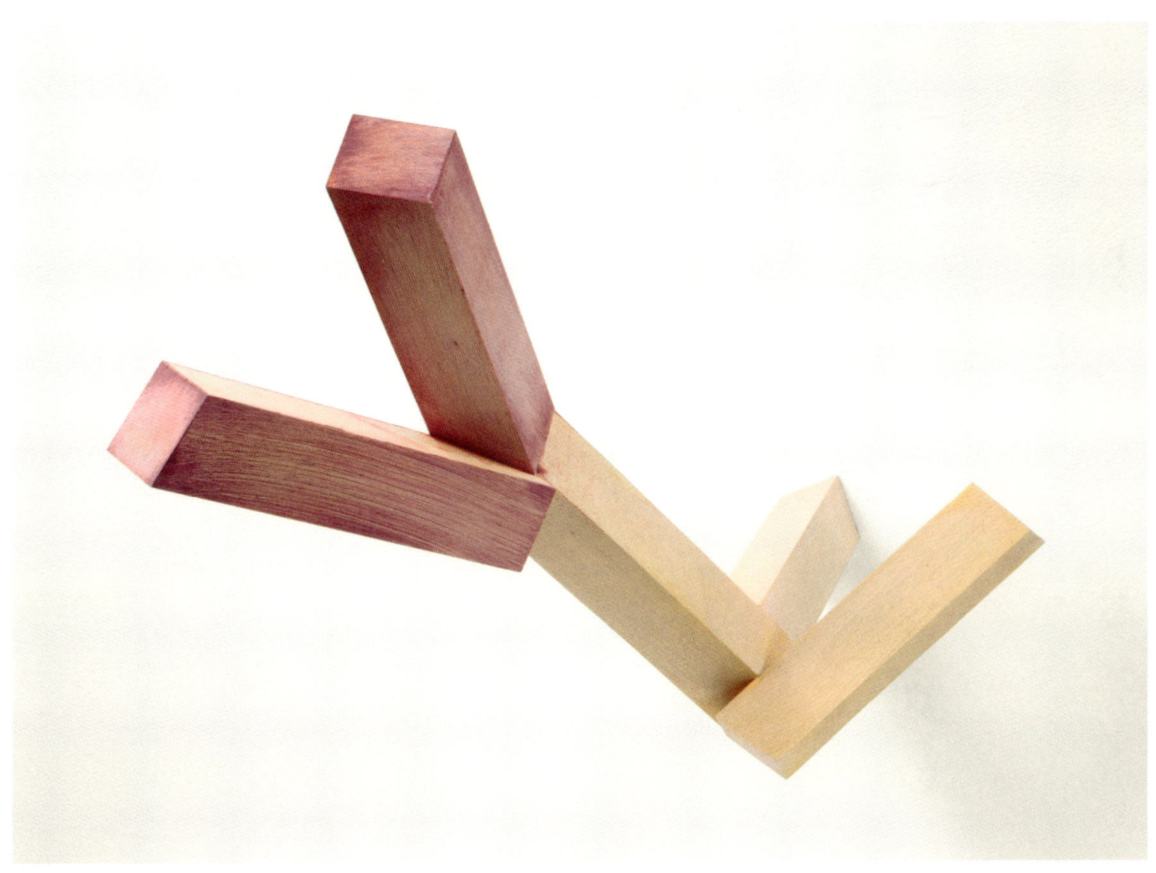

Untitled, 1997, oil paint on wood, 16 ³/₈ × 14 × 26"

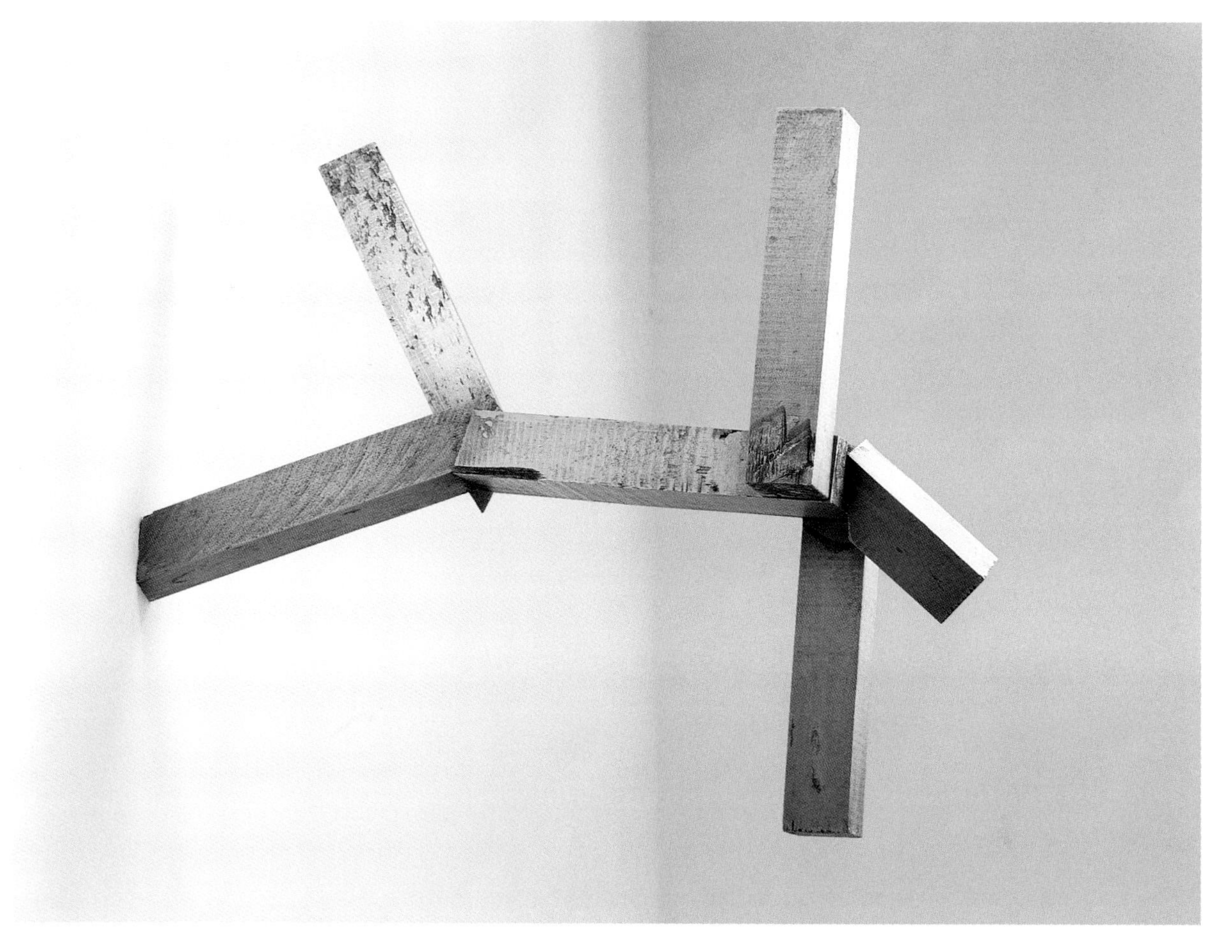

Untitled, 1997-98, white bronze, 17 $^1/_8$ × 13 $^1/_2$ × 21 $^1/_4$", unique

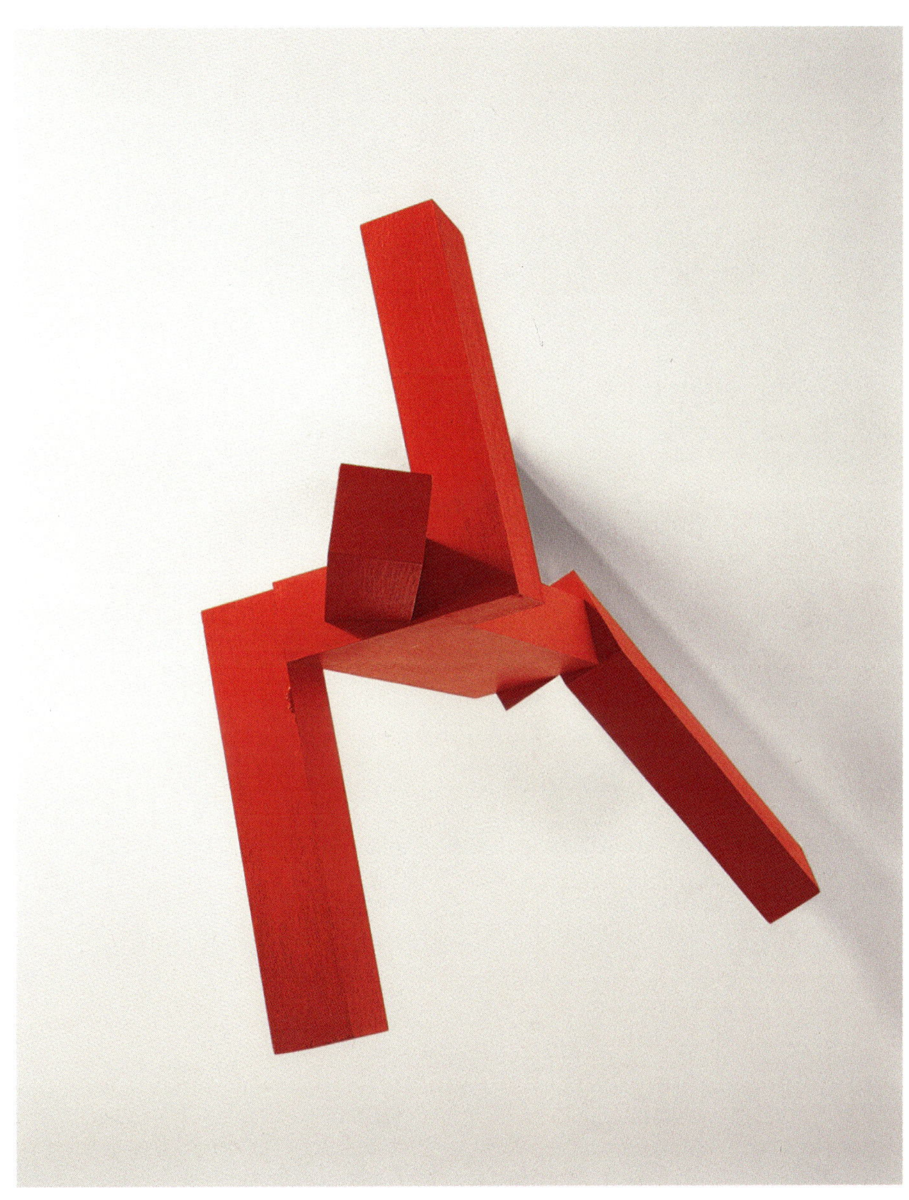

Untitled, 1997, oil paint on wood, 22 x 19 x 29"

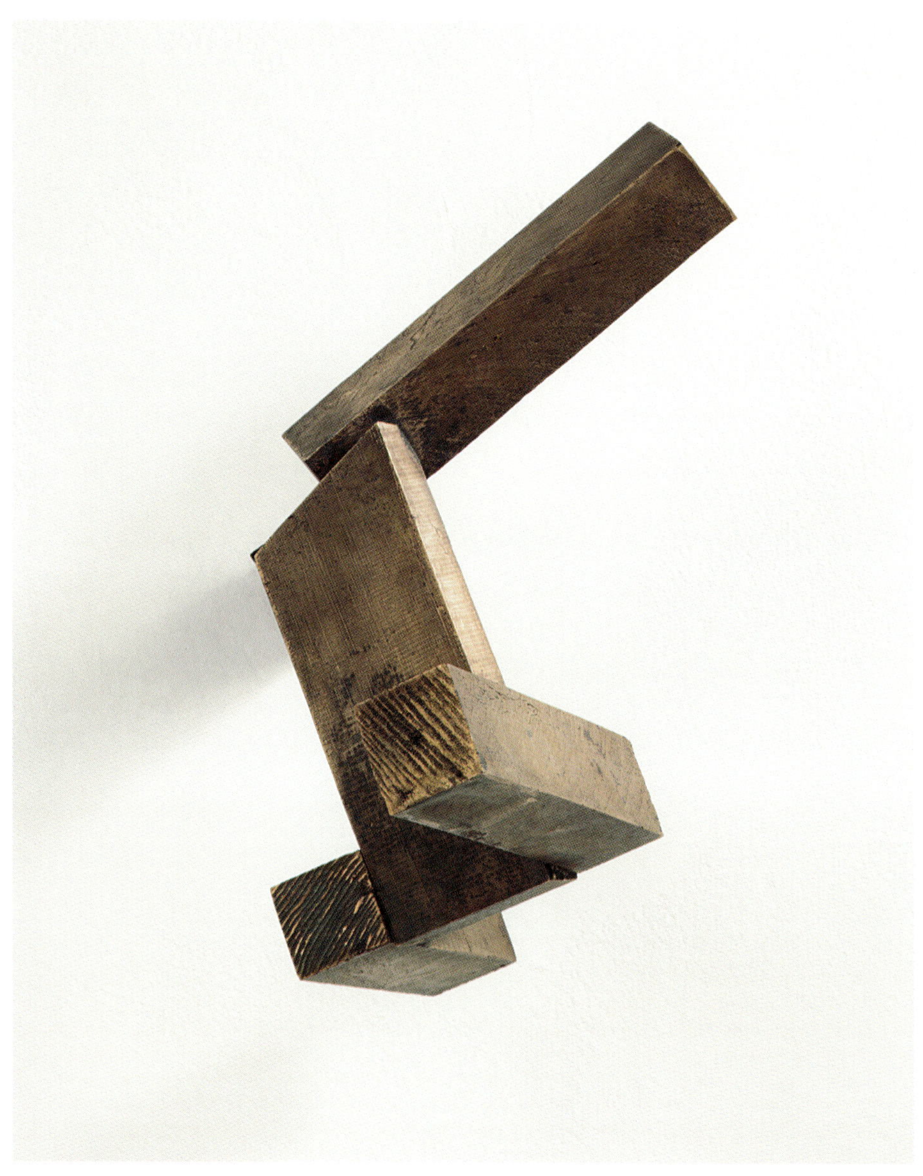

Untitled, 1997-98, copper, 14 $^{1}/_{2}$ × 6 $^{3}/_{4}$ × 15 $^{1}/_{2}$", unique

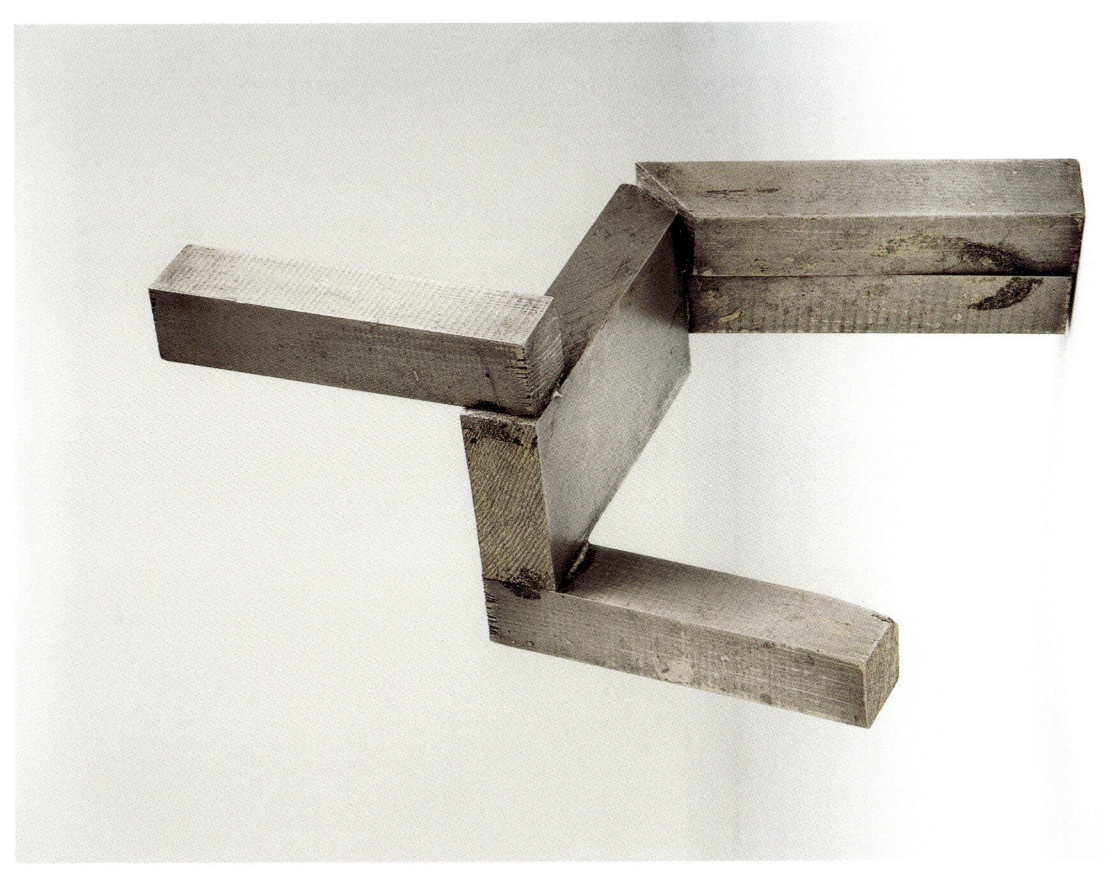

Untitled, 1997-98, bronze, 11 × 7 ¾ × 15 ¾", unique

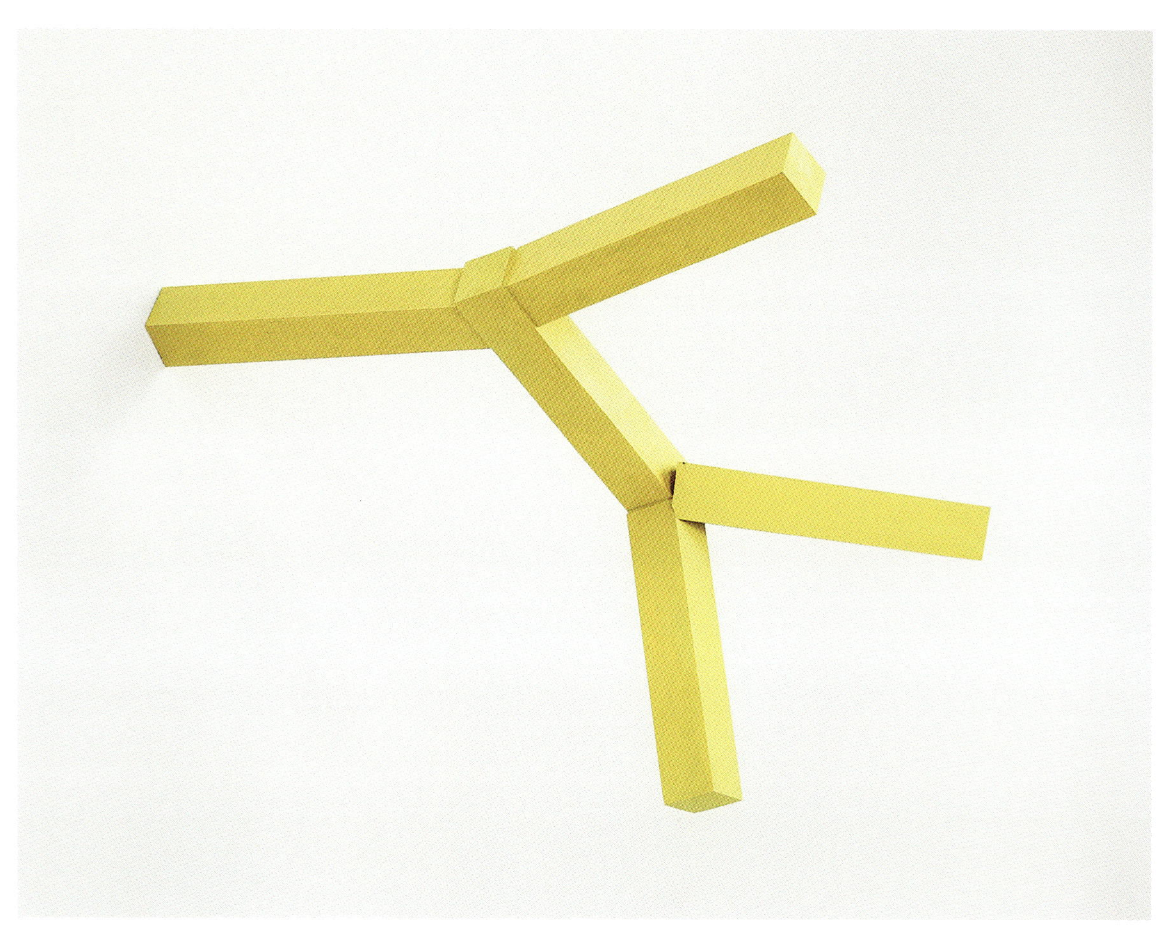

Untitled, 1997, oil paint on wood, $17\,^{7}/_{8} \times 11\,^{1}/_{2} \times 19\,^{1}/_{2}$"

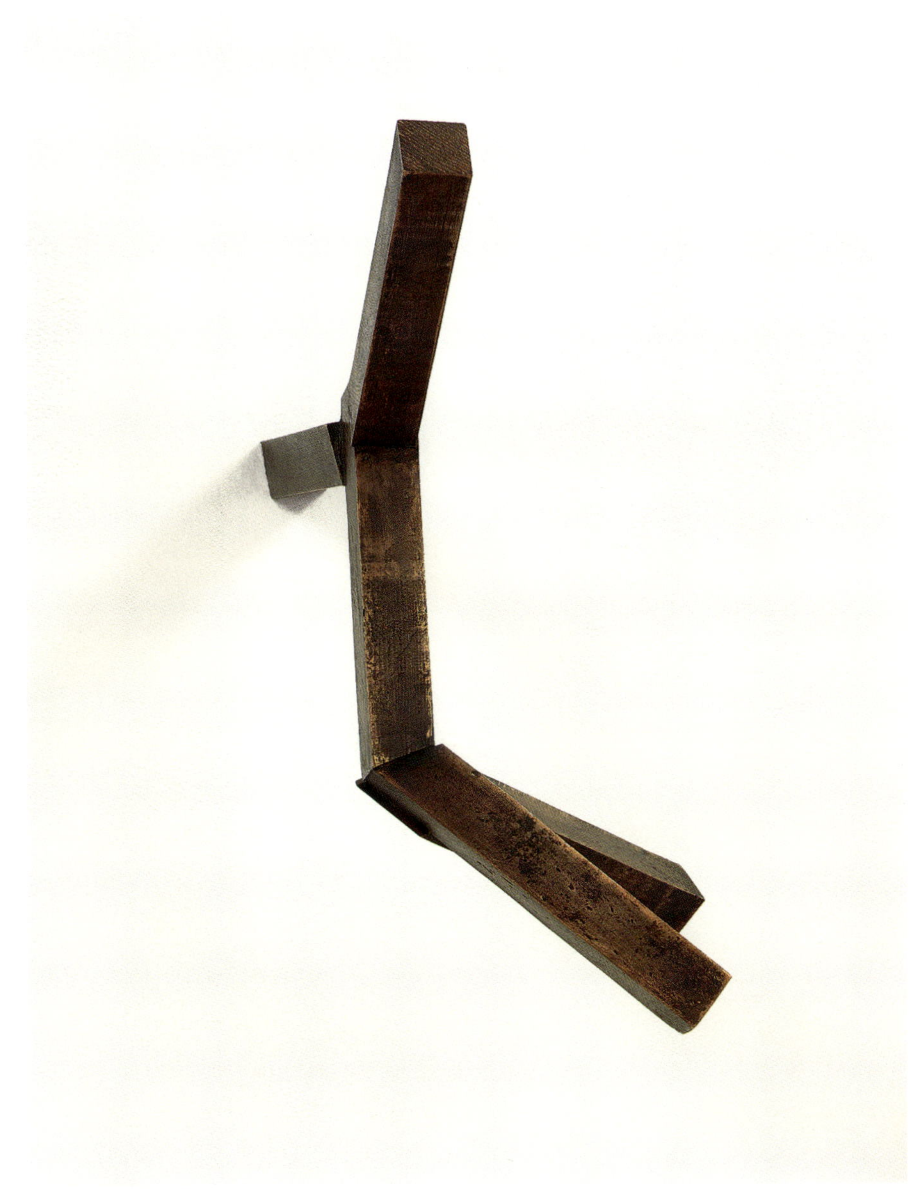

Untitled, 1998, copper, 18 3/8 × 9 3/4 × 16", unique

WORKS ILLUSTRATED IN CATALOGUE

cover: Untitled, 1997, oil paint on wood, 20 $\frac{1}{2}$ × 16 × 20 $\frac{1}{4}$"

9. Untitled, 1997, bronze, 87 × 58 $\frac{1}{2}$ × 31 $\frac{1}{2}$", unique

11. Untitled, 1997, bronze, 8' 6" × 12' × 10', edition 1/2

13. Untitled, 1997, bronze, 10' 6" × 21' 6" × 9', unique

15. Untitled, 1998, wood and steel, 67 × 24 × 21 $\frac{1}{2}$" variable

17. Untitled, 1998, wood and steel, 56 × 27 × 33"

19. Untitled, 1998, wood and steel, 79 × 58 × 30" variable

21. Untitled, 1998, wood, 94 $\frac{1}{2}$" × 9' 9" × 8' 2"

22. Untitled, 1998, bronze, 15 $\frac{1}{4}$ × 9 $\frac{3}{4}$ × 16 $\frac{3}{8}$", unique

23. Untitled, 1997, oil paint on wood, 15 × 22 $\frac{1}{2}$ × 25 $\frac{1}{2}$"

24. Untitled, 1997-98, bronze, 2 $\frac{3}{8}$ × 13 $\frac{1}{2}$ × 9 $\frac{1}{2}$", unique

25. Untitled, 1997, oil paint on aluminum, 18 $\frac{1}{2}$ × 18 $\frac{1}{2}$ × 16 $\frac{1}{4}$"

26. Untitled, 1997-98, oil paint on wood, 30 × 51 $\frac{1}{4}$ × 39"

27. Untitled, 1998, cast iron and white bronze, 9 × 16 × 18 $\frac{1}{2}$", cast iron; 9 × 12 $\frac{1}{2}$ × 18 $\frac{1}{2}$", white bronze

28. Untitled, 1997, oil paint on wood, 18 $\frac{1}{2}$ × 17 × 10 $\frac{1}{2}$"

29. Untitled, 1997, oil paint on wood, 24 $\frac{1}{2}$ × 38 $\frac{1}{2}$ × 24 $\frac{1}{2}$"

30. Untitled, 1997, aluminum, 21 × 9 × 20", unique

31. Untitled, 1998, oil paint on wood, 16 $\frac{3}{4}$ × 13 $\frac{1}{2}$ × 20 $\frac{1}{2}$"

32. Untitled, 1997, oil paint on wood, 22 $\frac{5}{8}$ × 16 $\frac{3}{8}$ × 17 $\frac{3}{8}$"

33. Untitled, 1997, oil paint on wood, 16 $\frac{3}{8}$ × 14 × 26"

34. Untitled, 1997-98, white bronze, 17 $\frac{1}{8}$ × 13 $\frac{1}{2}$ × 21 $\frac{1}{4}$", unique

35. Untitled, 1997, oil paint on wood, 22 × 19 × 29"

36. Untitled, 1997-98, copper, 14 $\frac{1}{2}$ × 6 $\frac{3}{4}$ × 15 $\frac{1}{2}$", unique

37. Untitled, 1997-98, bronze, 11 × 7 $\frac{3}{4}$ × 15 $\frac{3}{4}$", unique

38. Untitled, 1997, oil paint on wood, 17 $\frac{7}{8}$ × 11 $\frac{1}{2}$ × 19 $\frac{1}{2}$"

39. Untitled, 1998, copper, 18 $\frac{3}{8}$ × 9 $\frac{3}{4}$ × 16", unique

41. Untitled, 1998, wood, 15' 9" × 20' 8" × 91 $\frac{1}{2}$"

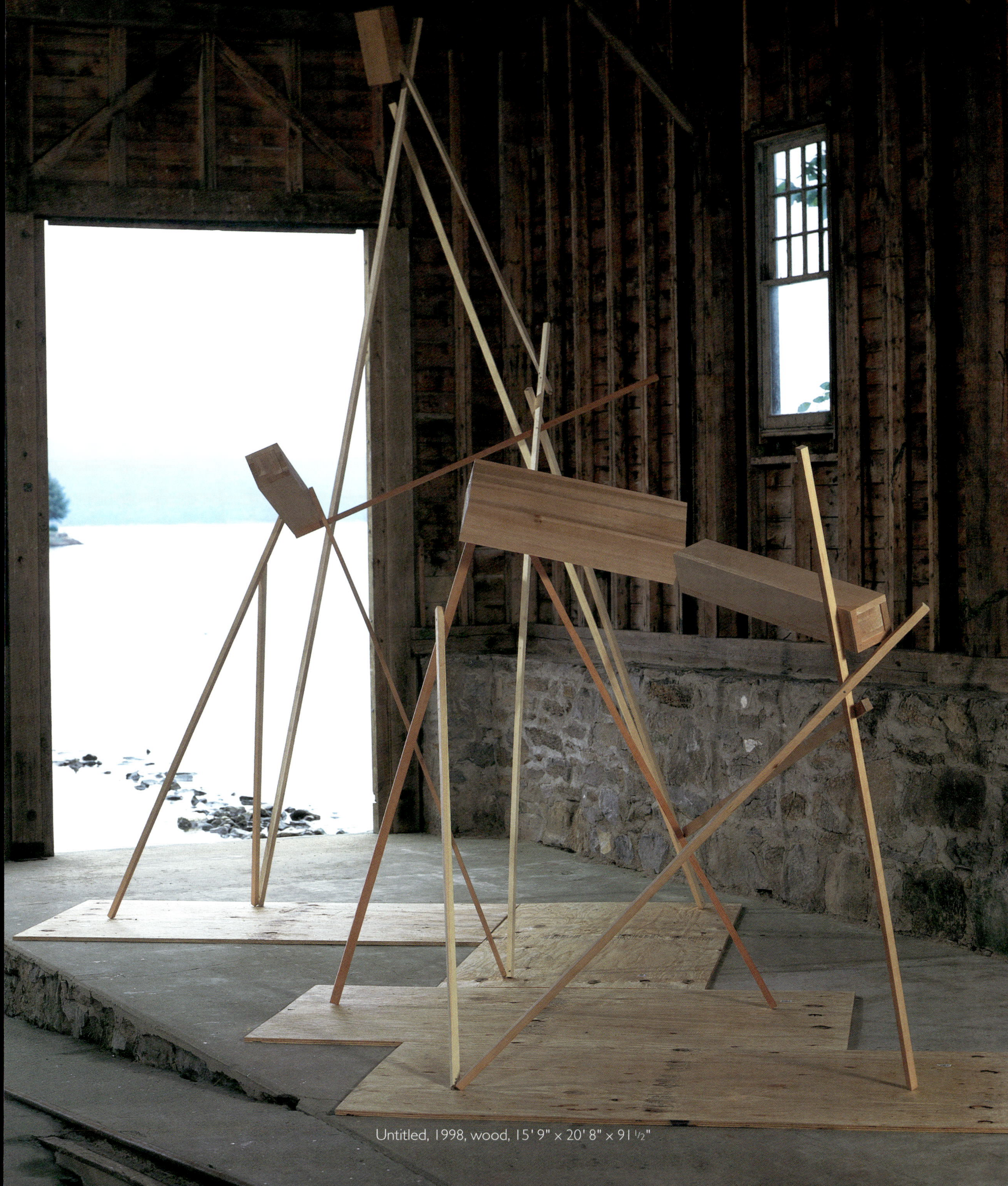

Untitled, 1998, wood, 15' 9" × 20' 8" × 91 ¹/₂"

Photography:
Ken Burris Studio; 15, 17, 19, 41
Gordon Riley Christmas; 23, 35
Oliver Heissner, Hamburg; back cover
Wilfred Petzi; 11, 13
Ellen Page Wilson; cover, 4-5, 9, 21, 22, 24-34, 36-39

Design and production:
Tomoko Makiura and Paul Pollard

ISBN: 1-878283-80-4